W9-AAY-793

TO BE A DEMOCRAT

COURAGE, PRINCIPLES & PROGRESS

★ ★ ★ ★ ★ ★ ★ ★ ★ ★ ★ ★ ★

Alice —

It's been a joy working with you. I hope your retirement is not too retiring.

Best Wishes

Mary Ellen

Mary Ellen Andriot Blencoe

ISBN: 978-1451543834

Harriman, Tennessee

For my family,
especially my grandchildren,
because that's what it's all about.

☆☆☆

All the ills of democracy can
be cured by more democracy.

Alfred E. Smith

ACKNOWLEDGEMENTS

My heartfelt thanks go to my husband Jim, my sons David and Greg, and my mother Jeanne Andriot for their enduring love and support. Other family members and friends who have inspired and encouraged me include my sisters Judy McLaughlin (who edited the book), Wendy Andriot, and Laurie Andriot (who indexed the book); my brother Jay Andriot; my daughter-in-law Becky Blencoe; friends Naida Finane (who critiqued the book) and Clint LaFollette (who shared the craft of bookbinding with me).

I dedicate this book to my granddaughters Catalina and Mary Jeanne, who are the lights of my life, and the memories of my father John Andriot, who encouraged me to walk in other's shoes, and my dear friend Eleanor Helton, who personified the Democratic spirit.

Contents

PRINCIPLES

Introduction

I have always been a Democrat. Growing up in the Virginia suburbs of Washington, D.C., politics was a part of daily life. In 1960 when I was in tenth grade, I voted for John F. Kennedy in a mock presidential election at McLean High School. Kennedy narrowly defeated Richard Nixon in this civics exercise, just as he did in the actual election. I was hooked.

My political memories of the intervening years are snapshots of the various campaigns. Being part of the crowd in 1964, cheering First Lady Ladybird Johnson as she boarded a train in Alexandria, Virginia, for a whistle-stop campaign tour. The energized optimism in 1968 when Robert F. Kennedy announced his candidacy, and the devastating anguish of his assassination. Telling my mother in 1984 that she should keep her eyes on a man for whom I was campaigning in Tennessee because I was sure he was going places – his name was Al Gore. Traveling with the Gore Corps in 1988 and 2000. Being on the Mall in Washington, D. C. during the Inaugural festivities in January 1993. The profound agony of the 2000 election fiasco. Listening to Barack Obama, a relative unknown state senator from Illinois, eloquently deliver the keynote address at the 2004 Democratic National Convention, and then just four years later, watching him take the oath of office of President of the United States. These events and many more made me feel a part of the political process and reaffirmed my decision to be a Democrat.

Exactly what is a Democrat? Why do people decide to be Democrats? What is the common thread that bonds us as Democrats?

Why is the Democratic Party so diverse? These questions came to my mind one summer evening as I, a liberal Democrat, listened to my congressman Lincoln Davis, a conservative Democrat, speak about our party's values. The concept of this book took root that day.

I originally envisioned the book as a collection of quotes from well-known contemporary Democrats in politics and show business. I mailed dozens of letters to such people asking them to explain why they were Democrats. The results were disappointing – I will be forever grateful to actor Edward Asner and Gov. John Baldacci of Maine, the only two individuals who responded.

Not to be deterred, I discovered that a vast array of letters, essays, and speeches by well-known Democrats was available in the public domain. In addition, the authors of other speeches graciously granted me permission to include their works in this book. The selections fell naturally into three categories – courage, principles, and progress – and are presented in chronological order within each category.

COURAGE: Throughout the history of the United States, courageous men and women have boldly spoken out on issues that were unpopular, controversial, or personally difficult. The Courage selections are examples of such bravery exhibited by elected officials and common citizens; by Native Americans, African Americans, and immigrants; by the very rich and the very poor.

PRINCIPLES: What did Thomas Jefferson, Andrew Jackson, and Harry Truman have in common? They all believed in an inclusive government in which the common people participated, rather than an exclusive government run by an aristocracy. The Principles selections define what it means to be a Democrat and describe the Democratic dream of a better life, a future in which opportunities are available to all, regardless of gender, race, ethnicity, religion, or sexual orientation.

PROGRESS: During the twentieth century, there were eight Democratic presidents: Woodrow Wilson, Franklin Roosevelt, Harry Truman, John Kennedy, Lyndon Johnson, Jimmy Carter, and Bill Clinton. It is not an exaggeration to say that significantly more progress was made in the areas of social security, civil rights, environmental protection, education, and the war on poverty during their administrations than those of the Republican presidents who held the office during that same time period. This section includes a speech given by each Democratic president in which he describes the major goals for his administration, followed by a list of the actual accomplishments of that administration. Democrats should be proud of this collective body of progressive legislation.

The first Democratic president of the twenty-first century, Barack Obama, took office on January 20, 2009. I have included his accomplishments so far, and am sure there will be many during the remainder of his presidency.

In compiling this book I became acquainted with people previously unknown to me and reacquainted with those with whom I was familiar. It was fascinating to discover that several major issues have been addressed repeatedly over the years. For instance, Robert LaFollette in 1917, Adlai Stevenson in 1952, and Russell Feingold in 2001 all spoke about preserving freedom of speech during a time of national crisis.

Some of the selections included in this book are not the words of Democrats. However, they do address issues that transcend party lines – religious freedom, equality, human rights, and freedom of speech.

To Be a Democrat illustrates the historical strengths of Democrats. It is my hope that it answers the questions which prompted its inception, and leads its readers to discover or rediscover why they are Democrats.

COURAGE

IT IS FROM NUMBERLESS DIVERSE ACTS OF COURAGE...THAT HUMAN HISTORY IS SHAPED. EACH TIME A MAN STANDS UP FOR AN IDEAL, OR ACTS TO IMPROVE THE LOT OF OTHERS, OR STRIKES OUT AGAINST INJUSTICE, HE SENDS FORTH A TINY RIPPLE OF HOPE, AND CROSSING EACH OTHER FROM A MILLION DIFFERENT CENTERS OF ENERGY AND DARING THOSE RIPPLES BUILD A CURRENT THAT CAN SWEEP DOWN THE MIGHTIEST WALLS OF OPPRESSION AND RESISTANCE.

Robert F. Kennedy
Capetown, South Africa
June 6, 1966

SAGOYEWATHA
(CHIEF RED JACKET)

Chief Red Jacket was the English name of a Native American chief of the Seneca tribe in the state of New York. His birth name, Otetiani, was changed to Sagoyewatha when he became chief. During the American Revolution, he was an ally of the British and wore one of their red uniform coats, hence his colorful nickname. He dealt skillfully with the white settlers, and was among the Native American chiefs who met with George Washington in 1792. Proud of his heritage, he resented the attempts of the European Americans to "civilize" his people, especially in regards to religion.

FROM HIS SPEECH DEFENDING NATIVE AMERICAN RELIGION 1805

Brother, listen to what we say. There was a time when our forefathers owned this great island. Their seats extended from the rising to the setting sun. The Great Spirit had made it for the use of Indians. He had created the buffalo, the deer, and other animals for food. He had made the bear and the beaver. Their skins served us for clothing. He had scattered them over the country, and taught us how to take them. He had caused the earth to produce corn for bread.... If we had some disputes about our hunting ground, they were generally settled without the shedding of much blood. But an evil day came upon us. Your forefathers crossed the great water and landed on this island. Their numbers were small. They found friends and not enemies. They told us they had fled from their own country for fear of wicked men, and had come here to enjoy their religion. They asked for a small seat. We took pity on them, granted their request; and they sat down amongst us. We gave them corn and meat; they gave us poison in return.

The white people, Brother, had now found our country. Tidings were carried back, and more came amongst us. Yet we did not fear them. We took them to be friends. They called us brothers. We believed them, and gave them a larger seat. At length their numbers had greatly increased. They wanted more land; they wanted our country. Our eyes were opened, and our minds became uneasy. Wars took place. Indians were hired to fight against Indians, and many of our people were destroyed. They also brought liquor amongst us. It was strong and powerful, and has slain thousands.

Brother, our seats were once large and yours were small. You have now become a great people, and we have scarcely a place left to spread our blankets. You have got our country, but are not satisfied; you want to force your religion upon us.

Brother, continue to listen. You say that you are sent to instruct us how to worship the Great Spirit agreeably to his mind, and, if we do not take hold of the religion which you white people teach, we shall be unhappy hereafter. You say that you are right and we are lost. How do we know this to be true? We…only know what you tell us about it. How shall we know when to believe, being so often deceived by the white people?

Brother, you say there is but one way to worship and serve the Great Spirit. If there is but one religion, why do you white people differ so much about it?

Brother, we do not understand these things. We are told that your religion was given to your forefathers, and has been handed down from father to son. We also have a religion, which was given to our forefathers, and has been handed down to us, their children. We worship in that way. It teaches us to be thankful for all the favours we receive; to love each other, and to be united. We never quarrel about religion.

Brother, the Great Spirit has made us all, but he has made a great difference between his white and red children. He has given us different complexions and different customs.… Since he has made so great a difference between us in other things, why may we not conclude that he has given us a different religion? Brother, we do not wish to destroy your religion, or take it from you. We only want to enjoy our own.

SUSAN B. ANTHONY

Susan B. Anthony, who was born in 1820, dedicated her life to the women's rights movement. She began in the temperance movement in the 1840's because of the abuse many women and children suffered from alcoholic men. As a woman, she was not allowed to speak at temperance rallies, and this led her to join Elizabeth Cady Stanton in campaigning for women's rights. During the 1850's, she was active in the American Anti-Slavery Society. Following the Civil War, she called for women to be granted the same rights given to black men in the Fourteenth and Fifteenth Amendments to the U.S. Constitution. In 1872, she was arrested and charged with voting illegally. From that time until her death in 1906, she spoke across the country, calling for a Constitutional amendment extending the right to vote to women. This right was finally granted when the Nineteenth Amendment, first proposed in 1878, was ratified in 1920, 14 years after Anthony's death.

FROM HER LECTURE ON WOMEN'S RIGHT TO VOTE 1873

Friends and fellow citizens: I stand before you tonight under indictment for the alleged crime of having voted at the last presidential election, without having a lawful right to vote. It shall be my work this evening to prove to you that in thus voting, I not only committed no crime, but, instead, simply exercised my citizen's rights, guaranteed to me and all United States citizens by the National Constitution, beyond the power of any state to deny.

The preamble of the Federal Constitution says:

> *We, the people of the United States, in order to form a more perfect union, establish justice, insure domestic tranquility, provide for the common defense, promote the general welfare, and secure the blessings of liberty to ourselves and our posterity, do ordain and establish this Constitution for the United States of America.*

It was we, the people; not we, the white male citizens; nor yet we, the male citizens; but we, the whole people, who formed the Union. And we formed it, not to give the blessings of liberty, but to secure them; not to the half of ourselves and the half of our posterity, but to the whole people – women as well as men. And it is a downright mockery to talk to women of their enjoyment of the blessings of liberty while they are denied the use of the only means of securing them provided by this democratic-republican government – the ballot.

For any state to make sex a qualification that must ever result in the disfranchisement of one entire half of the people, is to pass a bill of attainder, or an *ex post facto* law, and is therefore a violation of the supreme law of the land. By it the blessings of liberty are forever withheld from women and their female posterity.

To them this government has no just powers derived from the consent of the governed. To them this government is not a democracy. It is not a republic. It is an odious aristocracy; a hateful oligarchy of sex; the most hateful aristocracy ever established on the face of the globe; an oligarchy of wealth, where the rich govern the poor. An oligarchy of learning, where the educated govern the ignorant, or even an oligarchy of race, where the Saxon rules the African, might be endured; but this oligarchy of sex, which makes father, brothers, husband, sons, the oligarchs over the mother and sisters, the wife and daughters, of every household – which ordains all men sovereigns, all women subjects, carries dissension, discord, and rebellion into every home of the nation.

Webster, Worcester, and Bouvier all define a citizen to be a person in the United States, entitled to vote and hold office. The only question left to be settled now is: Are women persons? And I hardly believe any of our opponents will have the hardihood to say they are not. Being persons, then, women are citizens; and no state has a right to make any law, or to enforce any old law, that shall abridge their privileges or immunities. Hence, every discrimination against women in the constitutions and laws of the several states is today null and void, precisely as is every one against Negroes.

BOOKER T. WASHINGTON

Booker T. Washington, born a slave in 1856, earned money to pay for his education at the Hampton Institute in Virginia by working as a janitor. He became a teacher and in 1881 was asked to be the principal of a new school in Alabama, the Tuskegee Institute. In order to raise money for the school, he went on speaking tours across the nation, becoming well known as a result. His autobiography, Up From Slavery, *was a best-seller, and he was an advisor to President Theodore Roosevelt.*

FROM HIS SPEECH, "DEMOCRACY AND EDUCATION," TO THE INSTITUTE OF ARTS AND SCIENCES SEPTEMBER 30, 1896

My friends, we are one in this country. The question of the highest citizenship and the complete education of all concerns nearly ten million of my own people and over sixty million of yours. We rise as you rise; when we fall you fall. When you are strong we are strong; when we are weak you are weak. There is no power than can separate our destiny. The Negro can afford to be wronged; the white man cannot afford to wrong him.

If a white man steals a Negro's ballot, it is the white man who is permanently injured. Physical death comes to the one Negro lynched in a county, but death of the morals – death of the soul – comes to the thousands responsible for the lynching.

We are a patient, humble people. We can afford to work and wait. There is plenty in this country for us to do. Away up in the atmosphere of goodness, forbearance, patience, long-suffering, and forgiveness the workers are not many or overcrowded. If others would be little, we can be great. If others would be mean, we can be good. If others would push us down, we can help push them up. Character, not circumstances, makes the man....

During the next half-century and more my race must continue passing through the severe American crucible. We are to be tested in our patience, in our forbearance, our power to endure wrong, to withstand temptation, to succeed, to acquire and use skill, our ability to compete, to succeed in commerce; to disregard the superficial for the real, the appearance for the substance; to be great and yet the servant of all. This, this is the passport to all that is best in the life of our republic, and the Negro must possess it or be debarred. In working out our destiny, while the main burden and center of activity must be with us, we shall need in a large measure the help, the encouragement, the guidance that the strong can give the weak. Thus helped, we of both races in the South shall soon throw off the shackles of racial and sectional prejudice and rise above the clouds of ignorance, narrowness, and selfishness into that atmosphere, that pure sunshine, where it will be our highest ambition to serve man, our brother, regardless of race or past conditions.

FLORENCE KELLEY

The daughter of a U. S. congressman, Florence Kelley studied at Cornell University and the University of Zurich. In 1891, following an unsuccessful marriage, she and her three children moved to Chicago where she worked with Jane Addams and others at Hull House. Two years later, she was appointed by the Governor of Illinois as the first chief factory inspector. She was among those who founded the National Consumers League in 1899, whose main purpose was to establish a minimum wage and limit the working hours of women and children.

"CHILD LABOR AND WOMAN SUFFRAGE" SPEECH
PHILADELPHIA, PENNSYLVANIA
JULY 22, 1905

We have, in this country, two million children under the age of sixteen years who are earning their bread. They vary in age from six and seven years (in the cotton mills of Georgia) and eight, nine and ten years (in the coal-breakers of Pennsylvania), to fourteen, fifteen and sixteen years in more enlightened states.

No other portion of the wage earning class increased so rapidly from decade to decade as the young girls from fourteen to twenty years. Men increase, women increase, youth increase, boys increase in the ranks of the breadwinners; but no contingent so doubles from census period to census period (both by percent and by count of heads), as does the contingent of girls between twelve and twenty years of age. They are in commerce, in offices, in manufacturing.

Tonight while we sleep, several thousand little girls will be working in textile mills, all the night through, in the deafening noise of the spindles and the looms spinning and weaving cotton and wool, silks and ribbons for us to buy.

In Alabama the law provides that a child under sixteen years of age shall not work in a cotton mill at night longer than eight hours, and Alabama does better in this respect than any other southern state. North and South Carolina and Georgia place no restriction upon the work of children at night; and while we sleep, little white girls will be working tonight in the mills in those states, working eleven hours at night.

In Georgia there is no restriction whatever! A girl of six or seven years, just tall enough to reach the bobbins, may work eleven hours by day or by night. And they will do so tonight, while we sleep.

Nor is it only in the South that these things occur. Alabama does better than New Jersey. For Alabama limits the children's work at night to eight hours, while New Jersey permits it all night long. Last year New Jersey took a long backward step. A good law was repealed which had required women and children to stop work at six in the evening and at noon on Friday. Now, therefore, in New Jersey, boys and girls, after their 14th birthday, enjoy the pitiful privilege of working all night long.

In Pennsylvania, until last May it was lawful for children, 13 years of age, to work twelve hours at night. A little girl, on her thirteenth birthday, could start away from her home at half past five in the afternoon, carrying her pail of midnight luncheon as happier people carry their midday luncheon, and could work in the mill from six at night until six in the morning, without violating any law of the Commonwealth.

If the mothers and the teachers in Georgia could vote, would the Georgia Legislature have refused at every session for the last three years to stop the work in the mills of children under twelve years of age?

Would the New Jersey Legislature have passed that shameful repeal bill enabling girls of fourteen years to work all night, if the mothers in New Jersey were enfranchised? Until the mothers in the great industrial states are enfranchised, we shall none of us be able to free our consciences from participation in this great evil. No one in this room tonight can feel free from such participation. The children make our shoes in the shoe factories; they knit our stockings, our knitted underwear in the knitting factories. They spin and weave our cotton underwear in the cotton mills. Children braid straw for our hats, they spin and weave the silk and velvet wherewith we trim our hats. They stamp buckles and metal ornaments of all kinds, as well as pins and hat-pins. Under the sweating system, tiny children make artificial flowers and neckwear for us to buy. They carry bundles of garments from the factories to the tenements, little beasts of burden, robbed of school life that they may work for us.

We do not wish this. We prefer to have our work done by men and women. But we are almost powerless. Not wholly powerless, however, are citizens who enjoy the right of petition. For myself, I shall use this power in every possible way until the right to the ballot is granted, and then I shall continue to use both.

What can we do to free our consciences? There is one line of action by which we can do much. We can enlist the workingmen on behalf of our enfranchisement just in proportion as we strive with them to free the children. No labor organization in this country ever fails to respond to an appeal for help in the freeing of the children.

For the sake of the children, for the Republic in which these children will vote after we are dead, and for the sake of our cause, we should enlist the workingmen voters, with us, in this task of freeing the children from toil!

Robert M. LaFollette

Robert "Fighting Bob" LaFollette, a progressive Republican, served the state of Wisconsin as a U. S. congressman, governor, and U. S. senator. While governor, his notable legislation included the adoption of a primary election system (the first in the U. S.), railroad taxes based on property ownership, and taxes on corporations to raise money for the state budget. He also created a railroad commission, increased funding for education, and passed a civil service law. Elected to the U. S. Senate in 1904, LaFollette favored neutrality in World War I. He voted against American participation in the war, and protested the wartime limitations on speech and the press. His continued criticisms of the war, spawned efforts to expel him from the Senate. However, the 1918 elections gave the Republicans a single vote majority in the Senate, which made LaFollette a much needed member of his party. His bid for the presidency in 1924 as an independent Progressive led to his expulsion from the Republican Party conference. Ironically, in 1957 the Senate named him one of the five most outstanding senators of all time.

From His Address from the Floor of the U. S. Senate on Free Speech in Wartime October 6, 1917

I think all men recognize that in time of war the citizen must surrender some rights for the common good which he is entitled to enjoy in time of peace. But sir, the right to control their own Government according to constitutional forms is not one of the rights that the citizens of this country are called upon to surrender in time of war.

Rather in time of war the citizen must be more alert to the preservation of his right to control his Government. He must be most watchful of the encroachment of the military upon the civil power. He must beware of those precedents in support of arbitrary action by administration officials which, excused on the plea of necessity in war time, become the fixed rule when the necessity has passed and normal conditions have been restored.

More than all, the citizen and his representative in Congress in time of war must maintain his right of free speech. More than in times of peace it is necessary that the channels for free public discussion of governmental policies shall be open and unclogged. I believe, Mr. President, that I am now touching upon the most important question in this country today – and that is the right of the citizens of this country and their representatives in Congress to discuss in an orderly way frankly and publicly and without fear, from the platform and through the press, every important phase of this war; its causes, and manner in which it should be conducted, and the terms upon which peace should be made. The belief which is becoming widespread in this land, that this most fundamental right is being denied to the citizens of this country is a fact, the tremendous significance of which those in authority have not yet begun to appreciate. I am contending, Mr. President, for the great fundamental right of the sovereign people of this country to make their voice heard and have that voice heeded upon the great questions arising out of this war, including not only how the war shall be prosecuted but the conditions upon which it may be terminated with a due regard for the rights and the honor of this Nation and the interests of humanity.

Eleanor Roosevelt

Due to her controversial and outspoken stands on many issues, Eleanor Roosevelt was one of the most admired women in the world, as well as one of the most unpopular. A member of the Junior League, Consumer's League, League of Women Voters, and Women's Trade Union League, she constantly sought to improve the lives of the underprivileged. She attended her first Democratic National Convention in 1912, joined the Women's Division of the New York Democratic State Committee in 1922, and was appointed director of the Bureau of Women's Activities by the Democratic National Committee in 1928. As First Lady, she participated in many of President Roosevelt's programs and published a daily syndicated column, My Day. *Following the death of her husband and the end of World War II, she served in the United Nations and continued her work in the areas of human and civil rights.*

From Her Speech to the American Civil Liberties Union March 14, 1940

"Civil Liberties" emphasizes the liberty of the individual. In many other forms of governments the importance of the individual has disappeared. The individual lives for the state. Here in a democracy, the government still exists for the individual, but that does not mean that we do not have to watch and that we do not have to examine ourselves to be sure that we preserve the civil liberties for all our people, which are the basis of our democracy.

Now, you know if we are honest with ourselves, in spite of all we have said, in spite of our Constitution, many of us in this country do not enjoy real liberty. For that reason we know that everywhere in this country every person who believes in democracy has come to feel a real responsibility to work in his community and to know the people of his community, and to take the trouble to try to bring about the full observance of all our people of their civil liberties....

Any citizen in this country is entitled to equality before the law; to equality of education; to equality at earning a living, as far as his abilities have made it possible for him to do; to equality of participation in government so that he or she may register their opinion in just the way that any other citizens do. Now those things are basic rights, belonging to every citizen in every minority group, and we have an obligation, I think, to stand up and be counted when it comes to the question of whether any minority group does not have those rights as citizens in this country. The minute we deny any rights of this kind to any citizen, we are preparing the way for the denial of those rights to someone else. We have to make up our minds what we really believe. We have to decide whether we believe in the Bill of Rights, in the Constitution of the United States, or whether we are going to modify it because of the fears that we may have at the moment.

FRANKLIN D. ROOSEVELT

As Americans coped with the far-reaching effects of the Depression during the 1930's, repressive governments emerged in Germany, Italy, Russia, and Japan. Although the U. S. sought to be neutral, its allies in Europe were under attack and needed weapons and munitions. In his annual address to Congress in January 1941, President Franklin Roosevelt proposed the Lend-Lease Act, which would allow the U. S. to sell military equipment and materials to our allies, but defer payment until after the hostilities ended. He spoke of his belief that the U. S. should support "all of those resolute people everywhere who are resisting aggression and are thereby keeping war away from our hemisphere." In the same address he spoke of his vision of a future world and of four essential human freedoms upon which that world should be based. Eleven months later, the Japanese attacked Pearl Harbor, and the United States entered World War II.

FROM HIS ANNUAL ADDRESS TO CONGRESS
JANUARY 6, 1941

The Nation takes great satisfaction and much strength from the things which have been done to make its people conscious of their individual stake in the preservation of democratic life in America. Those things have toughened the fibre of our people, have renewed their faith and strengthened their devotion to the institutions we make ready to protect.

Certainly this is no time for any of us to stop thinking about the social and economic problems which are the root cause of the social revolution which is today a supreme factor in the world. For there is nothing mysterious about the foundations of a healthy and strong democracy. The basic things expected by our people of their political and economic systems are simple. They are:

- Equality of opportunity for youth and for others.

- Jobs for those who can work.
- Security for those who need it.
- The ending of special privilege for the few.
- The preservation of civil liberties for all.
- The enjoyment of the fruits of scientific progress in a wider and constantly rising standard of living.

These are the simple, basic things that must never be lost sight of in the turmoil and unbelievable complexity of our modern world. The inner and abiding strength of our economic and political systems is dependent upon the degree to which they fulfill these expectations.

Many subjects connected with our social economy call for immediate improvement. As examples:

- We should bring more citizens under the coverage of old-age pensions and unemployment insurance.
- We should widen the opportunities for adequate medical care.
- We should plan a better system by which persons deserving or needing gainful employment may obtain it.

I have called for personal sacrifice. I am assured of the willingness of almost all Americans to respond to that call.

A part of the sacrifice means the payment of more money in taxes. In my Budget Message I shall recommend that a greater portion of this great defense program be paid for from taxation than we are paying today. No person should try, or be allowed, to get rich out of this program; and the principle of tax payments in accordance with ability to pay should be constantly before our eyes to guide our legislation. If the Congress maintains these principles, the voters, putting patriotism ahead of pocketbooks, will give you their applause.In the future days, which we seek to make secure, we look forward to a world founded upon four essential human freedoms.

The first is freedom of speech and expression – everywhere in the world.

The second is freedom of every person to worship God in his own way – everywhere in the world.

The third is freedom from want – which, translated into world terms, means economic understandings which will secure to every nation a healthy peacetime life for its inhabitants – everywhere in the world.

The fourth is freedom from fear – which, translated into world terms, means a world-wide reduction of armaments to such a point and in such a thorough fashion that no nation will be in a position to commit an act of physical aggression against any neighbor – anywhere in the world.

That is no vision of a distant millennium. It is a definite basis for a kind of world attainable in our own time and generation. That kind of world is the very antithesis of the so-called new order of tyranny which the dictators seek to create with the crash of a bomb.

To that new order we oppose the greater conception – the moral order. A good society is able to face schemes of world domination and foreign revolutions alike without fear.

Since the beginning of our American history, we have been engaged in change – in a perpetual peaceful revolution – a revolution which goes on steadily, quietly adjusting itself to changing conditions – without the concentration camp or the quick-lime in the ditch. The world order which we seek is the cooperation of free countries, working together in a friendly, civilized society.

This nation has placed its destiny in the hands and heads and hearts of its millions of free men and women; and its faith in freedom under the guidance of God. Freedom means the supremacy of human rights everywhere. Our support goes to those who struggle to gain those rights or keep them. Our strength is our unity of purpose. To that high concept there can be no end save victory.

HUBERT H. HUMPHREY

Throughout his first term as President of the United States, Harry Truman's repeated call for civil rights legislation went unheeded by the Republicans and conservative Democrats in Congress. Truman wanted anti-lynching legislation, a guaranteed right to vote for all citizens, the elimination of the poll tax, and the end to discrimination in employment, interstate travel, and military service. At the 1948 Democratic National Convention, moderates headed by Minneapolis mayor and senatorial candidate Hubert H. Humphrey, proposed a strong civil rights plank in the platform based on the program Truman had been endorsing. There was a heated debate between the moderates and conservatives of the platform committee, but in the end the moderates prevailed. With Party leaders fearing a southern walkout, Humphrey addressed the convention as to why the time had come to extend civil rights. Although the convention approved the platform, it would be many years before civil rights legislation was enacted.

SPEAKING ON BEHALF OF THE MINORITY REPORT ON CIVIL RIGHTS TO THE DEMOCRATIC NATIONAL CONVENTION JULY 14, 1948

I realize that in speaking in behalf of the minority report on civil rights as presented by Congressman DeMiller of Wisconsin that I am dealing with a charged issue – with an issue which has been confused by emotionalism on all sides of the fence. I realize that there are here today friends and colleagues of mine, many of them, who feel just as deeply and keenly as I do about this issue and who are yet in complete disagreement with me.

My respect and admiration for these men and their views was great when I came to this convention. It is now far greater because of the sincerity, the courtesy, and the forthrightness with which many of them have argued in our prolonged discussions in the platform committee.

Because of this very great respect – and because of my profound belief that we have a challenging task to do here – because good conscience, decent morality, demands it – I feel I must rise at this time to support a report – the minority report – a report that spells out our democracy, a report that the people of this country can and will understand, and a report that they will enthusiastically acclaim on the great issue of civil rights!

Now let me say at the outset that this proposal is made for no single region. Our proposal is made with no single class, with no single racial or religious group in mind. All of the regions of this country, all of the states have shared in the precious heritage of American freedom. All the states and all the regions have seen at least some infringements of that freedom – all people – get this – all people, white and black, all groups, all racial groups have been the victims at times in this nation of – let me say – vicious discrimination.

The masterly statement of our keynote speaker, the distinguished United States Senator from Kentucky, Alben Barkley, made that point with great force. Speaking of the founder of our party, Thomas Jefferson, he said this, and I quote from Alben Barkley:

> *He did not proclaim that all the white, or the black, or the red, or the yellow men are equal; that all Christian or Jewish men are equal; that all Protestant and all Catholic men are equal; that all rich or poor men are equal; that all good and bad men are equal. What he declared was that all men are equal; and the equality which he proclaimed was the equality in the right to enjoy the blessings of free government in which they may participate and to which they have given their support.*

Now these words of Senator Barkley's are appropriate to this convention – appropriate to this convention of the oldest, the most truly progressive political party in America. From the time of Thomas Jefferson, the time of that immortal American doctrine of individual rights, under just and fairly administered laws, the Democratic Party has tried hard to secure expanding freedoms for all citizens. Oh, yes, I know, other political parties may have talked more about civil rights, but the Democratic Party has surely done more about civil rights.

We have made progress; we have made great progress in every part of this country. We've made great progress in the South; we've made it in the West, in the North, and in the East, but we must now focus the direction of that progress toward the realization of a full program of civil rights for all. This convention must set out more specifically the direction in which our party efforts are to go.

We can be proud that we can be guided by the courageous trail blazing of two great Democratic presidents. We can be proud of the fact that our great and beloved immortal leader Franklin Roosevelt gave us guidance. And we can be proud of the fact – we can be proud of the fact – that Harry Truman has had the courage to give to the people of America the new emancipation proclamation!

It seems to me, it seems to me, that the Democratic Party needs to make definite pledges of the kinds suggested in the confidence placed in it by the people of all races and all sections of this country.

Sure, we're here as Democrats. But my good friends, we're here as Americans; we're here as the believers in the principal and the ideology of democracy, and I firmly believe that as men concerned with our country's future, we must specify in our platform guarantees which we have mentioned in the minority report.

Yes, this is far more than a party matter. Every citizen has a stake in the emergence of the United States as a leader in a free world. That world is being challenged by the world of slavery. For us to play our part effectively, we must be in a morally sound position.

We can't use a double standard – there's no room for double standards in American politics – for measuring our own and other people's policies. Our demands for democratic practices in other lands will be no more effective than the guarantees of those practiced in our own country.

Friends, delegates, I do not believe that there can be any compromise on the guarantee of civil rights which I have mentioned in the minority report.

In spite of my desire for unanimous agreement on the entire platform, in spite of my desire to see everybody here in honest and unanimous agreement, there are some matters which I think must be stated clearly and without qualification. There can be no hedging – the newspaper headlines are wrong! There will be no hedging, and there will be no watering down – if you please – of the instruments and the principals of the civil-rights program!

To those who say, my friends, to those who say, that we are rushing this issue of civil rights, I say to them we are 172 years late! To those who say, to those who say this civil-rights program is an infringement on states' rights, I say this: the time has arrived in America for the Democratic Party to get out of the shadow of states' rights and walk forthrightly into the bright sunshine of human rights!

People, people – human beings – this is the issue of the 20th century. People of all kinds – all sorts of people – and these people are looking to America for leadership, and they're looking to America for precept and example.

My good friends – my fellow Democrats – I ask you for calm consideration of our historic opportunity....

Let us do forget the evil passions, the blindness of the past. In these times of world economic, political, and spiritual crisis, we cannot – we must not – turn from the path so plainly before us. That path has already led us through many valleys of the shadow of death.

Now is the time to recall those who were left on that path of American freedom.

For all of us here, for the millions who have sent us, for the whole two-billion members of the human family, our land is now, more than ever before, the last best hope on earth. I know that we can – I know that we shall – begin here the fuller and richer realization of that hope – that promise of a land where all men are truly free and equal, and each man uses his freedom and equality wisely and well.

My good friends, I ask my party, I ask the Democratic Party, to march down the high road of progressive democracy. I ask this convention, I ask this convention, to say in unmistakable terms that we proudly hail, and we courageously support, our President and leader Harry Truman in his great fight for civil rights in America.

ADLAI STEVENSON

Following World War II, a wave of anticommunism spread across the United States, creating the "Red Scare." There were loyalty tests for U. S. government employees, and the U. S. House Un-American Activities Committee investigated suspected communists. In 1949 Gov. Adlai E. Stevenson of Illinois was asked to give a deposition as a character witness regarding his relationship with Alger Hiss. Hiss had been accused of being a communist spy – a charge he denied – and was on trial for perjury. Stevenson had worked with Hiss in the early 1930's at the Agricultural Adjustment Administration, and he testified that Hiss' reputation was good. Hiss was eventually convicted of perjury, and Stevenson was thereafter linked by association to a convicted communist. In 1951, Stevenson vetoed an Illinois anti-subversion bill, knowing that he would be castigated for it, just as he had been for his Hiss deposition. The Democrats drafted a reluctant Stevenson to be their presidential candidate in 1952 against Gen. Dwight D. Eisenhower. During the election campaign, the Republicans, led by vice-presidential candidate Richard Nixon, Wisconsin Senator Joseph McCarthy, and FBI Director J. Edgar Hoover, vilified Stevenson for his alleged communist associations. He lost to Eisenhower in both the 1952 and 1956 elections. In 1961, President John Kennedy appointed him ambassador to the United Nations, where he served until his death in 1965.

FROM HIS "NATURE OF PATRIOTISM" SPEECH TO THE AMERICAN LEGION CONVENTION AUGUST 27, 1952

We talk a great deal about patriotism. What do we mean by patriotism in the context of our times? I venture to suggest that what we mean is a sense of national responsibility which will enable America to remain master of her power – to walk with it in serenity and wisdom, with self-respect and the respect to all mankind; a patriotism that puts country ahead of self; a patriotism which is not short, frenzied outbursts of emotion, but the tranquil and steady dedication of a lifetime. The dedication of a lifetime – these are words that are easy to utter, but this is a mighty assignment. For it is often easier to fight for principles than to live up to them.

Patriotism, I have said, means putting country before self. This is no abstract phrase, and unhappily, we find some things in American life today of which we cannot be proud. Consider the groups who seek to identify their special interests with the general welfare. I find it sobering to think that their pressures might one day be focused on me. I have resisted them before and I hope the Almighty will give me the strength to do so again and again. And I should tell you – my fellow Legionnaires – as I would tell all other organized groups, that I intend to resist pressures from veterans, too, if I think their demands are excessive or in conflict with the public interest, which must always be the paramount interest.

Let me suggest, incidentally, that we are rapidly becoming a nation of veterans. If we were all to claim a special reward for our service, beyond that to which specific disability of sacrifice has created a just claim, who would be left to pay the bill? After all, we are Americans first and veterans second, and the best maxim for any administration is still Jefferson's: "Equal rights for all, special privileges for none."

True patriotism, it seems to me, is based on tolerance and a large measure of humility.

There are men among us who use "patriotism" as a club for attacking other Americans. What can we say for the self-styled patriot who thinks that a Negro, a Jew, a Catholic, or a Japanese-American is less an American than he? That betrays the deepest article of our faith, the belief in individual liberty and equality, which has always been the heart and soul of the American idea.

What can we say for the man who proclaims himself a patriot – and then for political or personal reasons attacks the patriotism of faithful public servants? I give you, as a shocking example, the attacks which have been made on the loyalty and the motives of our great wartime Chief of Staff, General Marshall. To me this is the type of "patriotism" which is, in Dr. Johnson's phrase, "the last refuse of scoundrels."

The anatomy of patriotism is complex. But surely intolerance and public irresponsibility cannot be cloaked in the shinning armor of rectitude and righteousness. Nor can the denial of the right to hold ideas that are different – the freedom of man to think as he pleases. To strike freedom of the mind with the fist of patriotism is an old and ugly subtlety.

And the freedom of the mind, my friends, has served America well. The vigor of our political life, our capacity for change, our cultural, scientific and industrial achievements, all derive from free inquiry, from the free mind, from the imagination, resourcefulness and daring of men who are not afraid of new ideas. Most all of us favor free enterprise for business. Let us also favor free enterprise for the mind. For, in the last analysis, we would fight to the death to protect it. Why is it, then, that we are sometimes slow to detect, or are indifferent to, the dangers that beset it?

Many of the threats to our cherished freedoms in these anxious, troubled times arise, it seems to me, from a healthy apprehension about the communist menace within our country. Communism is abhorrent. It is strangulation of the individual; it is death for the soul. Americans who have surrendered to this misbegotten idol have surrendered their right to our trust. And there can be no secure place for them in our public life.

Yet, as I have said before, we must take care not to burn down the barn to kill the rats. All of us, and especially patriotic organizations of enormous influence like the American Legion, must be vigilant in protecting our birthright from its too zealous friends while protecting it from its evil enemies.

The tragedy of our day is the climate of fear in which we live, and fear breeds repression. Too often sinister threats to the Bill of

Rights, to freedom of the mind, are concealed under the patriotic cloak of anti-communism.

I could add, from my own experience, that it is never necessary to call a man a communist to make political capital. Those of us who have undertaken to practice the ancient but imperfect art of government will always make enough mistakes to keep our critics well supplied with standard ammunition. There is no need for poison gas.

Another feature of our current scene that I think invites a similar restraint is the recurrent attacks in some communities upon our public schools.

There is not justification for indiscriminate attacks on our schools, and the sincere, devoted, and by no means overpaid teachers who labor in them. If there are any communist teachers, of course they should be excluded, but the task is not one for self-appointed thought police or ill-informed censors. As a practical matter, we do not stop communist activity in this way. What we do is give the communists material with which to defame us. And we also stifle the initiative of teachers and depreciate the prestige of the teaching profession which should be as honorable and esteemed as any among us.

Let me now, in my concluding words, inquire with you how we may affirm our patriotism in the troubled yet hopeful years that are ahead.

The central concern of the American Legion – the ideal which holds it together – the vitality which animates it – is patriotism. And those voices which we have heard most clearly and which are best remembered in our public life have always had the accent of patriotism.

It was always accounted a virtue in a man to love his country. With us it is now something more than a virtue. It is a necessity, a condition of survival. When an American says that he loves his country, he means not only that he loves the New England hills, the prairies glistening in the sun, the wide and rising plains, the great mountains, and the sea. He means that he loves an inner air, an inner light in which freedom lives and in which a man can draw the breath of self-respect.

Men who have offered their lives for their country know that patriotism is not the fear of something; it is the love of something. Patriotism with us is not the hatred of Russia; it is the love of this Republic and of the ideal of liberty of man and mind in which it was born, and to which this Republic is dedicated.

With this patriotism – patriotism in its large and wholesome meaning – America can master its power and turn it to the noble cause of peace. We can maintain military power without militarism; political power without oppression; and moral power without compulsion or complacency.

The road we travel is long, but at the end lies the grail of peace. And in the valley of peace we see the faint outlines of a new world, fertile and strong. It is odd that one of the keys to abundance should have been handed to civilization on a platter of destruction. But the power of the atom to work evil gives only the merest hint of its power for good. I believe that man stands on the eve of his greatest day. I know, too, that that day is not a gift but a prize; that we shall not reach it until we have won it.

Legionnaires are united by memories of war. Therefore, no group is more devoted to peace. I say to you now that there is work to be done, that the difficulties and dangers that beset our path at home and abroad are incalculable. There is sweat and sacrifice; there is much of patience and quiet persistence in our horoscope. Perhaps the goal is not even for us to see in our lifetime.

But we are embarked on a great adventure. Let us proclaim our faith in the future of man. Of good heart and good cheer, faithful to ourselves and our traditions, we can lift the cause of freedom, the cause of free men, so high no power on earth can tear it down. We can pluck this flower, safety, from this nettle, danger. Living, speaking, like men – like Americans – we can lead the way to our rendezvous in a happy, peaceful world.

Thank you – and forgive me for imposing on you for so long.

MARTIN LUTHER KING, JR.

Birmingham, Alabama, in the early 1960's was one of the most racist, segregated cities in the United States. Rather than comply with court orders to integrate city parks and swimming pools, those facilities were closed to everyone. In April, 1963, when local African Americans were unable to make any progress in desegregating the city, Dr. Martin Luther King and the Southern Christian Leadership Conference decided to go to Birmingham and lead nonviolent demonstrations. On April 12, which was Good Friday, Dr. King and Rev. Ralph Abernathy were arrested while leading demonstrators in a march to City Hall. Eight white Alabama clergymen released a statement addressed to Dr. King in which they denounced his methods of civil disobedience, and called for action through the use of the courts and negotiations with local leaders. The Letter from Birmingham Jail, written on scraps of paper and smuggled out of the jail, was Dr. King's response to those clergymen.

FROM HIS LETTER FROM BIRMINGHAM JAIL
APRIL 16, 1963

I am in Birmingham because injustice is here. Just as the prophets of the eighth century B.C. left their villages and carried their "thus saith the Lord" far beyond the boundaries of their home towns, and just as the Apostle Paul left his village of Tarsus and carried the gospel of Jesus Christ to the far corners of the Greco-Roman world, so am I compelled to carry the gospel of freedom beyond my own home town. Like Paul, I must constantly respond to the Macedonian call for aid.

Moreover, I am cognizant of the interrelatedness of all communities and states. I cannot sit idly by in Atlanta and not be concerned about what happens in Birmingham. Injustice anywhere is a threat to justice everywhere. We are caught in an inescapable network of mutuality, tied in a single garment of destiny. Whatever affects one directly, affects all indirectly. Never again can we afford to live with the narrow, provincial "outside agitator" idea. Anyone who lives inside the United States can never be considered an outsider anywhere within its bounds.

You deplore the demonstrations taking place in Birmingham. But your statement, I am sorry to say, fails to express a similar concern for the conditions that brought about the demonstrations. I am sure that none of you would want to rest content with the superficial kind of social analysis that deals merely with effects and does not grapple with underlying causes. It is unfortunate that demonstrations are taking place in Birmingham, but it is even more unfortunate that the city's white power structure left the Negro community with no alternative.

In any nonviolent campaign there are four basic steps: collection of the facts to determine whether injustices exist; negotiation; self-purification; and direct action. We have gone through all these steps in Birmingham. There can be no gainsaying the fact that racial injustice engulfs this community. Birmingham is probably the most thoroughly segregated city in the United States. Its ugly record of brutality is widely known. Negroes have experienced grossly unjust treatment in the courts. There have been more unsolved bombings of Negro homes and churches in Birmingham than in any other city in the nation. These are the hard, brutal facts of the case. On the basis of these conditions, Negro leaders sought to negotiate with the city fathers. But the latter consistently refused to engage in good-faith negotiation.

Then, last September, came the opportunity to talk with leaders of Birmingham's economic community. In the course of the negotiations, certain promises were made by the merchants – for example, to remove the stores humiliating racial signs. On the basis of these promises, the Reverend Fred Shuttlesworth and the leaders of the Alabama Christian Movement for Human Rights agreed to a moratorium on all demonstrations. As the weeks and months went by, we realized that we were the victims of a broken promise. A few signs, briefly removed, returned; the others remained.

As in so many past experiences, our hopes had been blasted, and the shadow of deep disappointment settled upon us. We had no alternative except to prepare for direct action, whereby we would present our very bodies as a means of laying our case before the conscience of the local and the national community. Mindful of the difficulties involved, we decided to undertake a process of self-purification. We began a series of workshops on nonviolence, and we repeatedly asked ourselves: "Are you able to accept blows without retaliating?" "Are you able to endure the ordeal of jail?" We decided to schedule our direct-action program for the Easter season, realizing that except for Christmas, this is the main shopping period of the year. Knowing that a strong economic withdrawal program would be the by-product of direct action, we felt that this would be the best time to bring pressure to bear on the merchants for the needed change.

Then it occurred to us that Birmingham's mayoralty election was coming up in March, and we speedily decided to postpone action until after election day. When we discovered that the Commissioner of Public Safety, Eugene "Bull" Connor, had piled up enough votes to be in the run-off we decided again to postpone action until the day after the run-off so that the demonstrations could not be used to cloud the issues. Like many others, we waited to see Mr. Connor defeated, and to this end we endured postponement after postponement. Having aided in this community need, we felt that our direct-action program could be delayed no longer.

You may well ask: "Why direct action? Why sit-ins, marches and so forth? Isn't negotiation a better path?" You are quite right in calling for negotiation. Indeed, this is the very purpose of direct action. Nonviolent direct action seeks to create such a crisis and foster such a tension that a community which has constantly refused to negotiate is forced to confront the issue. It seeks so to dramatize the issue that it can no longer be ignored. My citing the creation of tension as part of the work of the nonviolent-resister may sound rather shocking. But I must confess that I am not afraid of the word *tension*. I have earnestly opposed violent tension, but there is a type of constructive, nonviolent tension which is necessary for growth. Just as Socrates felt that it was necessary to create a tension in the mind so that individuals could rise from the bondage of myths and half-truths to the unfettered realm of creative analysis and objective appraisal, we must see the need for nonviolent gadflies to create the kind of tension in society that will help men rise from the dark depths of prejudice and racism to the majestic heights of understanding and brotherhood.

The purpose of our direct-action program is to create a situation so crisis-packed that it will inevitably open the door to negotiation. I therefore concur with you in your call for negotiation. Too long has our beloved Southland been bogged down in a tragic effort to live in monologue rather than dialogue.

One of the basic points in your statement is that the action that I and my associates have taken in Birmingham is untimely. Some have asked: "Why didn't you give the new city administration time to act?" The only answer that I can give to this query is that the new Birmingham administration must be prodded about as much as the outgoing one, before it will act. We are sadly mistaken if we feel that the election of Albert Boutwell as mayor will bring the millennium to Birmingham. While Mr. Boutwell is a much more gentle person than Mr. Connor, they are both segregationists, dedicated to maintenance of the status quo. I have hope that Mr. Boutwell will be reasonable enough to see the futility of massive resistance to desegregation. But he will not see this without pressure from devotees of civil rights. My friends, I must say to you that we have not made a single gain [in] civil rights without determined legal and nonviolent pressure. Lamentably, it is an historical fact that privileged groups seldom give up their privileges voluntarily. Individuals may see the moral light and voluntarily give up their unjust posture; but, as Reinhold Niebuhr has reminded us, groups tend to be more immoral than individuals.

We know through painful experience that freedom is never voluntarily given by the oppressor; it must be demanded by the oppressed. Frankly, I have yet to engage in a direct-action campaign that was "well timed" in the view of those who have not suffered unduly from the disease of segregation. For years now I have heard the word *Wait!* It rings in the ear of every Negro with piercing familiarity. This *Wait* has almost always meant *Never*. We must come to see, with one of our distinguished jurists, that "justice too long delayed is justice denied."

We have waited for more than 340 years for our constitutional and God-given rights. The nations of Asia and Africa are moving with jet-like speed toward gaining political independence, but we stiff creep at horse-and-buggy pace toward gaining a cup of coffee at a lunch counter. Perhaps it is easy for those who have never felt the stinging dark of segregation to say, "Wait." But when you have seen vicious mobs lynch your mothers and fathers at will and drown your sisters and brothers at whim; when you have seen hate-filled policemen curse, kick and even kill your black brothers and sisters; when you see the vast majority of your twenty million Negro brothers smothering in an airtight cage of poverty in the midst of an affluent society; when you suddenly find your tongue twisted and your speech stammering as you seek to explain to your six-year-old daughter why she can't go to the public amusement park that has just been advertised on television, and see tears welling up in her eyes when she is told that Funtown is closed to colored children, and see ominous clouds of inferiority beginning to form in her little mental sky, and see her beginning to distort her personality by developing an unconscious bitterness toward white people; when you have to concoct an answer for a five-year-old son who is asking: "Daddy, why do white people treat colored people so mean?"; when you take a cross-county drive and find it necessary to sleep night after night in the uncomfortable corners of your automobile because no motel will accept you; when you are humiliated day in and day out by nagging signs reading *white* and *colored*; when your first name becomes *nigger*, your middle name becomes *boy* (however old you are) and your last name becomes *John*, and your wife and mother are never given the respected title *Mrs.*; when you are harried by day and haunted by night by the fact that you are a Negro, living constantly at tiptoe stance, never quite knowing what to expect next, and are plagued with inner fears and outer resentments; when you are forever fighting a degenerating sense of *nobodiness,* then you will understand why we find it difficult to wait. There comes a time when the cup of endurance runs over, and men are no longer willing to be plunged into the abyss of despair. I hope, sirs, you can understand our legitimate and unavoidable impatience.

STEWART UDALL

In the years following World War II, Americans became increasingly aware of the interrelationship of the world's ecosystems and the importance of conservation. This awareness was brought into focus in 1962 by Rachel Carson in her book, Silent Spring, *in which she discussed the effects of pesticides on plants and animals. The space program also contributed to the concept of global interconnectivity when pictures of the Earth from space were made public. Stewart Udall, the Secretary of the Interior under Presidents Kennedy and Johnson, was a committed conservationist who believed in the federal government's responsibility for safe-guarding the environment and protecting natural resources. He defended his then-controversial policies in his best-selling book,* The Quiet Crisis, *which was published in 1963. During Udall's eight years as head of Interior, the National Park System added four national parks, 56 national wildlife areas, and established the first national seashore and Great Lakes parks. In addition, Congress passed the Wilderness Act, the Endangered Species Act, the Wild and Scenic Rivers Act, and the Land and Water Conservation Fund Act. He continued his work as an author, lawyer and conservation advocate until his death at the age of 90 in 2010.*

FROM HIS SPEECH, "THE CONSERVATION CHALLENGE OF THE SIXTIES," TO THE SCHOOL OF FORESTRY, UNIVERSITY OF CALIFORNIA, BERKELEY APRIL 19, 1963

A year ago President John F. Kennedy, in his March 1 [1962] special conservation message to Congress – the first presidential message of its kind in many years to be delivered to the Congress – undertook to do something that no other president has attempted; namely, to define the word "conservation." Conservation is difficult to define because it is a dynamic and constantly changing concept. But the President wrote in his message: "Conservation...can be defined as the wise use of our natural environment: it is, in the final analysis, the highest form of national thrift – the prevention of waste and despoilment while preserving, improving and renewing the quality and usefulness of all our resources." A little more than fifty years ago our dictionaries did not contain the word "conservation." The word, like the concept for which it stood, grew out of the ruminations of Gifford Pinchot and some of his friends. They applied it first to the idea of saving our forests and using them wisely. It was later applied to water and to minerals and it now, if we can see it properly, is a concept so broad in scope that it includes all of our dealings with natural resources and with our total environment as well.

If the forester and the reclamation engineer symbolized the conservation effort during Theodore Roosevelt's time, and the TVA planner and the CCC tree planter typified the New Deal, the swift ascendancy of technology has made the scientist the symbol of the sixties: his ultimate instruments, the reactor and the rocket, have opened the door to an inexhaustible storehouse of energy and may yet reveal the secrets of the stars. I think a historical look at the subject of conservation would reveal an ebb and flow, with two high tides in conservation, one under Theodore Roosevelt and one under his cousin Franklin. Some of us would like to think, although this depends upon you and others like you, that we are on the verge of the third wave.

For the first time in history a note of optimism pervades the resource reports of our experts. Conservation, we are told, is now largely a problem of efficient management. Most scarcities will be the result of poor planning or inadequate research. The central difference, in conservation, between the New Deal and the New Frontier, seems to relate to the dominance of scientific research and science-oriented planning in resource management. Science and technology hold the keys to the kingdom of abundance – and planning, long a favorite whipping-boy of "practical" men, is now the one indispensable science. Aided by the men of science, in some resource sectors we have reversed our course: we produce more, waste less, and make the needs of the future an integral part of our computations. We will no longer be able to explain away our shortcomings by pleading ignorance or incapacity. We have the insight and the power to conserve, and the existence of what I will call "areas of quiet crisis in resource management" indicts us, separately and collectively, for our failure to act. The quiet crisis in conservation in our country today is most acute when we consider our total outdoor environment. The assault on things natural has been massive during the past two decades. This has been perhaps the most significant conservation fact of the past generation. If it continues unimpeded, the face of the land and our relationship with it will be drastically and irrevocably altered. Our fascination with the dazzling things of an inventive era has seemingly diminished our love for the land. This trend has, of course, been quickened by the emphasis on urbanization and mobility, the seductions of spectatorship, the requirements of industrial growth, and the air-conditioned advantages that have made glassed-in living so appealing. It is understandable that, in hectic times, a sedentary and city-bound people would witness the erosion of outdoor resources without alarm.

But let us not mistake it. The deterioration of our environment has been the paramount conservation failure of the postwar years....Beset on every side by problems of growth and the pressures of progress, the American earth is fast losing its spaciousness and freshness and green splendor. We have grown too fast to grow wisely, and the inspiriting parts of our land will be irreparably mutilated unless we make environment planning and environment preservation urgent items of public business.

JOHN F. KENNEDY

Birmingham, Alabama was the focus of the civil rights movement in May 1963. After police and firemen used police dogs and high pressure fire hoses to disperse black protesters marching to end segregation in that city, President Kennedy attempted to effect change through negotiation. The violence escalated and Kennedy decided he must send Congress a major civil rights bill. On June 11th, he announced this decision in a televised address to the nation, and the following week sent the proposed bill to Congress. Tragically, he did not live to see the bill become law.

RADIO AND TELEVISION REPORT TO THE AMERICAN PEOPLE ON CIVIL RIGHTS JUNE 11, 1963

Good evening my fellow citizens:

This afternoon, following a series of threats and defiant statements, the presence of Alabama National Guardsmen was required on the University of Alabama to carry out the final and unequivocal order of the United States District Court of the Northern District of Alabama. That order called for the admission of two clearly qualified young Alabama residents who happened to have been born Negro.

That they were admitted peacefully on the campus is due in good measure to the conduct of the students of the University of Alabama, who met their responsibilities in a constructive way.

I hope that every American, regardless of where he lives, will stop and examine his conscience about this and other related incidents. This Nation was founded by men of many nations and backgrounds. It was founded on the principle that all men are created equal, and that the rights of every man are diminished when the rights of one man are threatened.

Today we are committed to a worldwide struggle to promote and protect the rights of all who wish to be free. And when Americans are sent to Vietnam or West Berlin, we do not ask for whites only. It ought to be possible, therefore, for American students of any color to attend any public institution they select without having to be backed up by troops.

It ought to be possible for American consumers of any color to receive equal service in places of public accommodation, such as hotels and restaurants and theaters and retail stores, without being forced to resort to demonstrations in the street, and it ought to be possible for American citizens of any color to register to vote in a free election without interference or fear of reprisal.

It ought to be possible, in short, for every American to enjoy the privileges of being American without regard to his race or his color. In short, every American ought to have the right to be treated as he would wish to be treated, as one would wish his children to be treated. But this is not the case.

The Negro baby born in America today, regardless of the section of the Nation in which he is born, has about one-half as much chance of completing a high school as a white baby born in the same place on the same day, one-third as much chance of completing college, one-third as much chance of becoming a professional man, twice as much chance of becoming unemployed, about one-seventh as much chance of earning $10,000 a year, a life expectancy which is seven years shorter, and the prospects of earning only half as much.

This is not a sectional issue. Difficulties over segregation and discrimination exist in every city, in every State of the Union, producing in many cities a rising tide of discontent that threatens the public safety. Nor is this a partisan issue. In a time of domestic crisis men of good will and generosity should be able to unite regardless of party or politics. This is not even a legal or legislative issue alone. It is better to settle these matters in the courts than on the streets, and new laws are needed at every level, but law alone cannot make men see right.

We are confronted primarily with a moral issue. It is as old as the scriptures and is as clear as the American Constitution.

The heart of the question is whether all Americans are to be afforded equal rights and equal opportunities, whether we are going to treat our fellow Americans as we want to be treated. If an American, because his skin is dark, cannot eat lunch in a restaurant open to the public, if he cannot send his children to the best public school available, if he cannot vote for the public officials who will represent him, if, in short, he cannot enjoy the full and free life which all of us want, then who among us would be content to have the color of his skin changed and stand in his place? Who among us would then be content with the counsels of patience and delay?

One hundred years of delay have passed since President Lincoln freed the slaves, yet their heirs, their grandsons, are not fully free. They are not yet freed from the bonds of injustice. They are not yet freed from social and economic oppression. And this Nation, for all its hopes and all its boasts, will not be fully free until all its citizens are free.

We preach freedom around the world, and we mean it, and we cherish our freedom here at home, but are we to say to the world, and much more importantly, to each other that this is the land of the free except for the Negroes; that we have no second-class citizens except Negroes; that we have no class or caste system, no ghettoes, no master race except with respect to Negroes?

Now the time has come for this Nation to fulfill its promise. The events in Birmingham and elsewhere have so increased the cries for equality that no city or State or legislative body can prudently choose to ignore them.

The fires of frustration and discord are burning in every city, North and South, where legal remedies are not at hand. Redress is sought in the streets, in demonstrations, parades, and protests which create tensions and threaten violence and threaten lives.

We face, therefore, a moral crisis as a country and as a people. It cannot be met by repressive police action. It cannot be left to increased demonstrations in the streets. It cannot be quieted by token moves or talk. It is time to act in the Congress, in your State and local legislative body and, above all, in all of our daily lives.

It is not enough to pin the blame on others, to say this is a problem of one section of the country or another, or deplore the fact that we face. A great change is at hand, and our task, our obligation, is to make that revolution, that change, peaceful and constructive for all.

Those who do nothing are inviting shame as well as violence. Those who act boldly are recognizing right as well as reality.

Next week I shall ask the Congress of the United States to act, to make a commitment it has not fully made in this century to the proposition that race has no place in American life or law. The Federal judiciary has upheld that proposition in the conduct of its affairs, including the employment of Federal personnel, the use of Federal facilities, and the sale of federally financed housing.

But there are other necessary measures which only the Congress can provide, and they must be provided at this session. The old code of equity law under which we live commands for every wrong a remedy, but in too many communities, in too many parts of the country, wrongs are inflicted on Negro citizens and there are no remedies at law. Unless the Congress acts, their only remedy is in the street.

I am, therefore, asking the Congress to enact legislation giving all Americans the right to be served in facilities which are open to the public – hotels, restaurants, theaters, retail stores, and similar establishments.

This seems to me to be an elementary right. Its denial is an arbitrary indignity that no American in 1963 should have to endure, but many do.

I have recently met with scores of business leaders urging them to take voluntary action to end this discrimination and I have been encouraged by their response, and in the last two weeks over 75 cities have seen progress made in desegregating these kinds of facilities. But many are unwilling to act alone, and for this reason, nationwide legislation is needed if we are to move this problem from the streets to the courts.

I am also asking the Congress to authorize the Federal Government to participate more fully in lawsuits designed to end segregation in public education. We have succeeded in persuading many districts to desegregate voluntarily. Dozens have admitted Negroes without violence. Today a Negro is attending a State-supported institution in every one of our 50 States, but the pace is very slow.

Too many Negro children entering segregated grade schools at the time of the Supreme Court's decision nine years ago will enter segregated high schools this fall, having suffered a loss which can never be restored. The lack of an adequate education denies the Negro a chance to get a decent job.

The orderly implementation of the Supreme Court decision, therefore, cannot be left solely to those who may not have the economic resources to carry the legal action or who may be subject to harassment.

Other features will also be requested, including greater protection for the right to vote. But legislation, I repeat, cannot solve this problem alone. It must be solved in the homes of every American in every community across our country.

In this respect I want to pay tribute to those citizens North and South who have been working in their communities to make life better for all. They are acting not out of a sense of legal duty but out of a sense of human decency.

Like our soldiers and sailors in all parts of the world they are meeting freedom's challenge on the firing line, and I salute them for their honor and their courage.

My fellow Americans, this is a problem which faces us all – in every city of the North as well as the South. Today there are Negroes unemployed, two or three times as many compared to whites, inadequate in education, moving into the large cities, unable to find work, young people particularly out of work without hope, denied equal rights, denied the opportunity to eat at a restaurant or lunch counter or go to a movie theater, denied the right to a decent education, denied almost today the right to attend a State university even though qualified. It seems to me that these are matters which concern us all, not merely Presidents or Congressmen or Governors, but every citizen of the United States.

This is one country. It has become one country because all of us and all the people who came here had an equal chance to develop their talents.

We cannot say to 10 percent of the population that you can't have that right; that your children cannot have the chance to develop whatever talents they have; that the only way that they are going to get their rights is to go into the streets and demonstrate. I think we owe them and we owe ourselves a better country than that.

Therefore, I am asking for your help in making it easier for us to move ahead and to provide the kind of equality of treatment which we would want ourselves; to give a chance for every child to be educated to the limit of his talents.

As I have said before, not every child has an equal talent or an equal ability or an equal motivation, but they should have an equal right to develop their talent and their ability and their motivation, to make something of themselves.

We have a right to expect that the Negro community will be responsible, will uphold the law, but they have a right to expect that the law will be fair, that the Constitution will be color blind, as Justice Harlan said at the turn of the century.

This is what we are talking about and this is a matter which concerns this country and what it stands for, and in meeting it I ask the support of all our citizens.

Thank you very much.

LYNDON B. JOHNSON

In early 1965, Lyndon Johnson was in the midst of preparing a voting rights bill, which he planned to introduce to Congress in the spring of 1966. At the same time, several civil rights organizations were attempting to register African Americans to vote, a right that had effectively been denied to a vast majority of them. To publicize this effort, a peaceful march from Selma to Montgomery, Alabama was planned. On March 7, a group of marchers, led by activists John Lewis and Hosea Williams, began the 50 mile walk. When they reached the Edmond Pettus Bridge in Selma, many of the marchers were assaulted by state troopers and deputies wielding tear gas and billy clubs. The event, which was well documented by photographers and journalists, became known as Bloody Sunday. Dr. Martin Luther King, Jr. came to Selma two days later and led a prayer at the Pettus Bridge. Demonstrations protesting the marchers' treatment were held in many other cities, and the White House and Congress were inundated with calls and letters from constituents. As a result, Lyndon Johnson addressed the issue in a televised joint session of Congress, and mobilized the National Guard to protect 25,000 demonstrators led by Dr. King and other celebrities as they finally completed the four-day journey. The Voting Rights Act was passed and signed into law that same year.

"The American Promise," Special Message to the Congress March 15, 1965

I speak tonight for the dignity of man and the destiny of democracy. I urge every member of both parties, Americans of all religions and of all colors, from every section of this country, to join me in that cause.

At times history and fate meet at a single time in a single place to shape a turning point in man's unending search for freedom. So it was at Lexington and Concord. So it was a century ago at Appomattox. So it was last week in Selma, Alabama. There, long-suffering men and women peacefully protested the denial of their rights as Americans. Many were brutally assaulted. One good man, a man of God, was killed.

There is no cause for pride in what has happened in Selma. There is no cause for self-satisfaction in the long denial of equal rights of millions of Americans. But there is cause for hope and for faith in our democracy in what is happening here tonight. For the cries of pain and the hymns and protests of oppressed people have summoned into convocation all the majesty of this great government – the government of the greatest nation on earth. Our mission is at once the oldest and the most basic of this country: to right wrong, to do justice, to serve man.

In our time we have come to live with the moments of great crisis. Our lives have been marked with debate about great issues – issues of war and peace, issues of prosperity and depression. But rarely in any time does an issue lay bare the secret heart of America itself. Rarely are we met with a challenge, not to our growth or abundance, or our welfare or our security, but rather to the values, and the purposes, and the meaning of our beloved nation. The issue of equal rights for American Negroes is such an issue.

And should we defeat every enemy, and should we double our wealth and conquer the stars, and still be unequal to this issue, then we will have failed as a people and as a nation. For with a country as with a person, "What is a man profited, if he shall gain the whole world, and lose his own soul?"

There is no Negro problem. There is no Southern problem. There is no Northern problem. There is only an American problem. And we are met here tonight as Americans – not as Democrats or Republicans. We are met here as Americans to solve that problem.

This was the first nation in the history of the world to be founded with a purpose. The great phrases of that purpose still sound in every American heart, North and South: "All men are created equal," "government by consent of the governed," "give me liberty or give me death." Well, those are not just clever words, or those are not just empty theories. In their name Americans have fought and died for two centuries, and tonight around the world they stand there as guardians of our liberty, risking their lives.

Those words are a promise to every citizen that he shall share in the dignity of man. This dignity cannot be found in a man's possessions; it cannot be found in his power, or in his position. It really rests on his right to be treated as a man equal in opportunity to all others. It says that he shall share in freedom, he shall choose his leaders, educate his children, provide for his family according to his ability and his merits as a human being. To apply any other test – to deny a man his hopes because of his color, or race, or his religion, or the place of his birth is not only to do injustice, it is to deny America and to dishonor the dead who gave their lives for American freedom.

Our fathers believed that if this noble view of the rights of man was to flourish, it must be rooted in democracy. The most basic right of all was the right to choose your own leaders. The history of this country, in large measure, is the history of the expansion of that right to all of our people. Many of the issues of civil rights are very complex and most difficult. But about this there can and should be no argument.

Every American citizen must have an equal right to vote.

There is no reason which can excuse the denial of that right. There is no duty which weighs more heavily on us than the duty we have to ensure that right.

Yet the harsh fact is that in many places in this country, men and women are kept from voting simply because they are Negroes. Every device of which human ingenuity is capable has been used to deny this right. The Negro citizen may go to register only to be told that the day is wrong, or the hour is late, or the official in charge is absent. And if he persists, and if he manages to present himself to the registrar, he may be disqualified because he did not spell out his middle name or because he abbreviated a word on the application. And if he manages to fill out an application, he is given a test. The registrar is the sole judge of whether he passes this test. He may be asked to recite the entire Constitution, or explain the most complex provisions of State law. And even a college degree cannot be used to prove that he can read and write.

For the fact is that the only way to pass these barriers is to show a white skin. Experience has clearly shown that the existing process of law cannot overcome systematic and ingenious discrimination. No law that we now have on the books – and I have helped to put three of them there – can ensure the right to vote when local officials are determined to deny it. In such a case our duty must be clear to all of us. The Constitution says that no person shall be kept from voting because of his race or his color. We have all sworn an oath before God to support and to defend that Constitution. We must now act in obedience to that oath.

Wednesday, I will send to Congress a law designed to eliminate illegal barriers to the right to vote. The broad principles of that bill will be in the hands of the Democratic and Republican leaders tomorrow. After they have reviewed it, it will come here formally as a bill. I am grateful for this opportunity to come here tonight at the invitation of the leadership to reason with my friends, to give them my views, and to visit with my former colleagues. I've had prepared a more comprehensive analysis of the legislation which I had intended to transmit to the clerk tomorrow, but which I will submit to the clerks tonight. But I want to really discuss with you now, briefly, the main proposals of this legislation.

This bill will strike down restrictions to voting in all elections – Federal, State, and local – which have been used to deny Negroes the right to vote. This bill will establish a simple, uniform standard which cannot be used, however ingenious the effort, to flout our Constitution. It will provide for citizens to be registered by officials of the United States Government, if the State officials refuse to register them. It will eliminate tedious, unnecessary lawsuits which delay the right to vote. Finally, this legislation will ensure that properly registered individuals are not prohibited from voting.

I will welcome the suggestions from all of the Members of Congress – I have no doubt that I will get some – on ways and means to strengthen this law and to make it effective. But experience has plainly shown that this is the only path to carry out the command of the Constitution.

To those who seek to avoid action by their National Government in their own communities, who want to and who seek to maintain purely local control over elections, the answer is simple:

- Open your polling places to all your people.
- Allow men and women to register and vote whatever the color of their skin.
- Extend the rights of citizenship to every citizen of this land.

There is no constitutional issue here. The command of the Constitution is plain. There is no moral issue. It is wrong – deadly wrong – to deny any of your fellow Americans the right to vote in this country. There is no issue of States' rights or national rights. There is only the struggle for human rights. I have not the slightest doubt what will be your answer.

But the last time a President sent a civil rights bill to the Congress, it contained a provision to protect voting rights in Federal elections. That civil rights bill was passed after eight *long* months of debate. And when that bill came to my desk from the Congress for my signature, the heart of the voting provision had been eliminated. This time, on this issue, there must be no delay, or no hesitation, or no compromise with our purpose.

We cannot, we must not, refuse to protect the right of every American to vote in every election that he may desire to participate in. And we ought not, and we cannot, and we must not wait another eight months before we get a bill. We have already waited a hundred years and more, and the time for waiting is gone.

So I ask you to join me in working long hours – nights and weekends, if necessary – to pass this bill. And I don't make that request lightly. For from the window where I sit with the problems of our country, I recognize that from outside this chamber is the outraged conscience of a nation, the grave concern of many nations, and the harsh judgment of history on our acts.

But even if we pass this bill, the battle will not be over. What happened in Selma is part of a far larger movement which reaches into every section and State of America. It is the effort of American Negroes to secure for themselves the full blessings of American life. Their cause must be our cause too. Because it's not just Negroes, but really it's all of us, who must overcome the crippling legacy of bigotry and injustice.

And we shall overcome.

As a man whose roots go deeply into Southern soil, I know how agonizing racial feelings are. I know how difficult it is to reshape the attitudes and the structure of our society. But a century has passed, more than a hundred years since the Negro was freed. And he is not fully free tonight.

It was more than a hundred years ago that Abraham Lincoln, a great President of another party, signed the Emancipation Proclamation; but emancipation is a proclamation, and not a fact. A century has passed, more than a hundred years, since equality was promised. And yet the Negro is not equal. A century has passed since the day of promise. And the promise is un-kept.

The time of justice has now come. I tell you that I believe sincerely that no force can hold it back. It is right in the eyes of man and God that it should come. And when it does, I think that day will brighten the lives of every American. For Negroes are not the only victims. How many white children have gone uneducated? How many white families have lived in stark poverty? How many white lives have been scarred by fear, because we've wasted our energy and our substance to maintain the barriers of hatred and terror?

And so I say to all of you here, and to all in the nation tonight, that those who appeal to you to hold on to the past do so at the cost of denying you your future.

This great, rich, restless country can offer opportunity and education and hope to all, all black and white, all North and South, sharecropper and city dweller. These are the enemies: poverty, ignorance, disease. They're our enemies, not our fellow man, not our neighbor. And these enemies too – poverty, disease, and ignorance: we shall overcome.

Now let none of us in any section look with prideful righteousness on the troubles in another section, or the problems of our neighbors. There's really no part of America where the promise of equality has been fully kept. In Buffalo as well as in Birmingham, in Philadelphia as well as Selma, Americans are struggling for the fruits of freedom. This is one nation. What happens in Selma or in Cincinnati is a matter of legitimate concern to every American. But let each of us look within our own hearts and our own communities, and let each of us put our shoulder to the wheel to root out injustice wherever it exists.

As we meet here in this peaceful, historic chamber tonight, men from the South, some of whom were at Iwo Jima, men from the North who have carried Old Glory to far corners of the world and brought it back without a stain on it, men from the East and from the West, are all fighting together without regard to religion, or color, or region, in Vietnam. Men from every region fought for us across the world twenty years ago.

And now in these common dangers and these common sacrifices, the South made its contribution of honor and gallantry no less than any other region in the Great Republic – and in some instances, a great many of them, more.

And I have not the slightest doubt that good men from everywhere in this country, from the Great Lakes to the Gulf of Mexico, from the Golden Gate to the harbors along the Atlantic, will rally now together in this cause to vindicate the freedom of all Americans.

For all of us owe this duty; and I believe that all of us will respond to it. Your President makes that request of every American.

The real hero of this struggle is the American Negro. His actions and protests, his courage to risk safety and even to risk his life, have awakened the conscience of this nation. His demonstrations have been designed to call attention to injustice, designed to provoke change, designed to stir reform. He has called upon us to make good the promise of America. And who among us can say that we would have made the same progress were it not for his persistent bravery, and *his* faith in American democracy.

For at the real heart of battle for equality is a deep seated belief in the democratic process. Equality depends not on the force of arms or tear gas but depends upon the force of moral right; not on recourse to violence but on respect for law and order.

And there have been many pressures upon your President and there will be others as the days come and go. But I pledge you tonight that we intend to fight this battle where it should be fought – in the courts, and in the Congress, and in the hearts of men.

We must preserve the right of free speech and the right of free assembly. But the right of free speech does not carry with it, as has been said, the right to holler fire in a crowded theater. We must preserve the right to free assembly. But free assembly does not carry with it the right to block public thoroughfares to traffic.

We do have a right to protest, and a right to march under conditions that do not infringe the constitutional rights of our neighbors. And I intend to protect all those rights as long as I am permitted to serve in this office.

We will guard against violence, knowing it strikes from our hands the very weapons which we seek: progress, obedience to law, and belief in American values.

In Selma, as elsewhere, we seek and pray for peace. We seek order. We seek unity. But we will not accept the peace of stifled rights, or the order imposed by fear, or the unity that stifles protest. For peace cannot be purchased at the cost of liberty.

In Selma tonight – and we had a good day there – as in every city, we are working for a just and peaceful settlement And we must all remember that after this speech I am making tonight, after the police and the FBI and the Marshals have all gone, and after you have promptly passed this bill, the people of Selma and the other cities of the Nation must still live and work together. And when the attention of the nation has gone elsewhere, they must try to heal the wounds and to build a new community.

This cannot be easily done on a battleground of violence, as the history of the South itself shows. It is in recognition of this that men of both races have shown such an outstandingly impressive responsibility in recent days – last Tuesday, again today.

The bill that I am presenting to you will be known as a civil rights bill. But, in a larger sense, most of the program I am recommending is a civil rights program. Its object is to open the city of hope to all people of all races.

Because all Americans just must have the right to vote. And we are going to give them that right. All Americans must have the privileges of citizenship – regardless of race. And they are going to have those privileges of citizenship – regardless of race.

But I would like to caution you and remind you that to exercise these privileges takes much more than just legal right. It requires a trained mind and a healthy body. It requires a decent home, and the chance to find a job, and the opportunity to escape from the clutches of poverty.

Of course, people cannot contribute to the nation if they are never taught to read or write, if their bodies are stunted from hunger, if their sickness goes untended, if their life is spent in hopeless poverty just drawing a welfare check. So we want to open the gates to opportunity. But we're also going to give all our people, black and white, the help that they need to walk through those gates.

My first job after college was as a teacher in Cotulla, Texas, in a small Mexican-American school. Few of them could speak English, and I couldn't speak much Spanish. My students were poor and they often came to class without breakfast, hungry. And they knew, even in their youth, the pain of prejudice. They never seemed to know why people disliked them. But they knew it was so, because I saw it in their eyes. I often walked home late in the afternoon, after the classes were finished, wishing there was more that I could do. But all I knew was to teach them the little that I knew, hoping that it might help them against the hardships that lay ahead.

And somehow you never forget what poverty and hatred can do when you see its scars on the hopeful face of a young child. I never thought then, in 1928, that I would be standing here in 1965. It never even occurred to me in my fondest dreams that I might have the chance to help the sons and daughters of those students and to help people like them all over this country.

But now I do have that chance – and I'll let you in on a secret – I mean to use it. And I hope that you will use it with me.

This is the richest and the most powerful country which ever occupied this globe. The might of past empires is little compared to ours. But I do not want to be the President who built empires, or sought grandeur, or extended dominion.

I want to be the President who educated young children to the wonders of their world.

I want to be the President who helped to feed the hungry and to prepare them to be tax-payers instead of tax-eaters.

I want to be the President who helped the poor to find their own way and who protected the right of every citizen to vote in every election.

I want to be the President who helped to end hatred among his fellow men, and who promoted love among the people of all races and all regions and all parties.

I want to be the President who helped to end war among the brothers of this earth.

And so, at the request of your beloved Speaker, and the Senator from Montana, the majority leader, the Senator from Illinois, the minority leader, Mr. McCulloch, and other Members of both parties, I came here tonight – not as President Roosevelt came down one time, in person, to veto a bonus bill, not as President Truman came down one time to urge the passage of a railroad bill – but I came down here to ask you to share this task with me, and to share it with the people that we both work for. I want this to be the Congress, Republicans and Democrats alike, which did all these things for all these people.

Beyond this great chamber, out yonder in fifty States, are the people that we serve. Who can tell what deep and unspoken hopes are in their hearts tonight as they sit there and listen. We all can guess, from our own lives, how difficult they often find their own pursuit of happiness, how many problems each little family has. They look most of all to themselves for their futures. But I think that they also look to each of us.

Above the pyramid on the great seal of the United States it says in Latin: “God has favored our undertaking.” God will not favor everything that we do. It is rather our duty to divine His will.But I cannot help believing that He truly understands and that He really favors the undertaking that we begin here tonight.

ROBERT F. KENNEDY

Opposing the escalation of the Vietnam War, Senator Robert F. Kennedy announced his candidacy for the presidency of the United States on March 16, 1968. With the strong showing of antiwar candidate Senator Eugene McCarthy in the New Hampshire primary four days earlier, Kennedy believed he had a chance to defeat President Johnson. While ending the war in Vietnam was the primary issue of his campaign, Senator Kennedy also sought to improve the lives of the poor and minorities. His campaign lasted less than three months. Late in the evening of June 4, just minutes after delivering his victory speech for his win in the California primary, he was shot by Sirhan Sirhan. Doctors were unable to save his life, and he died on June 6, 1968.

From His Remarks at the University of Kansas March 18, 1968

I have seen children in Mississippi starving, their bodies so crippled by hunger; and their minds have been so destroyed for their whole life that they will have no future. I have seen children in Mississippi – here in the United States – with a gross national product of eight hundred billion dollars – I have seen children in the Delta area of Mississippi with distended stomachs, whose faces are covered with sores from starvation, and we haven't developed a policy so that we can get enough food so that they can live, so that their children, so that their lives are not destroyed. I don't think that's acceptable in the United States of America and I think we need a change.

I have seen Indians living on their bare and meager reservations, with no jobs, with an unemployment rate of 80 percent, and with so little hope for the future, so little left for the future that for young people, that for young men and women in their teens, the greatest cause of death is suicide. That they end their lives by killing themselves – I don't think that we have to accept that – for the first Americans, for this minority here in the United States. If young boys and girls are so filled with despair when they are going to high school and feel that their lives are so hopeless and that nobody's going to care for them, nobody's going to be involved with them, and nobody's going to bother with them, that they either hang themselves, shoot themselves, or kill themselves – I don't think that's acceptable and I think the United States of America – I think the American people, I think we can do much, much better.

And I run for the presidency because of that. I run for the presidency because I've seen proud men in the hills of Appalachia, who wish only to work in dignity, but they cannot, for the mines have closed and their jobs are gone and no one – neither industry, nor labor, nor government – has cared enough to help. I think we here in this country, with the unselfish spirit that exists in the United States of America, I think we can do better here also.

I have seen the people of the black ghetto, listening to ever-greater promises of equality and justice, as they sit in the same decaying schools and huddle in the same filthy rooms – without heat – warding off the cold and warding off the rats.

If we believe that we, as Americans, are bound together by a common concern for each other, then an urgent national priority is upon us. We must begin to end the disgrace of this other America.

And this is one of the great tasks of leadership for us, as individuals and citizens this year. But even if we act to erase material poverty, there is another great task. It is to confront the poverty of satisfaction – purpose and dignity – that inflicts us all. Too much and for too long, we seemed to have surrendered personal excellence and community values in the mere accumulation of material things. Our Gross National Product, now, is over $800 billion dollars a year, but that Gross National Product – if we judge the United States of America by that – counts air pollution and cigarette advertising, and ambulances to clear our highways of carnage. It counts special locks for our doors and the jails for those who break them. It counts the destruction of the redwood, and the loss of our natural wonder in chaotic sprawl. It counts napalm and counts nuclear warheads, and armored cars for police to fight riots in our cities. It counts Whitman's rifle and Speck's knife, and the television programs which glorify violence in order to sell toys to our children.

Yet the gross national product does not allow for the health of our children, the quality of their education, or the joy of their play. It does not include the beauty of our poetry or the strength of our marriages; the intelligence of our public debate or the integrity of our public officials. It measures neither our wit nor our courage; neither our wisdom nor our learning; neither our compassion nor our devotion to our country; it measures everything, in short, except that which makes life worthwhile. And it can tell us everything about America except why we are proud that we are American. . . .

If this is true here at home, so it is true elsewhere in the world. From the beginning, our proudest boast has been the promise of Jefferson, that we, here in this country, would be the best hope for all mankind. And now, as we look at the war in Vietnam, we wonder if we still hold a decent respect for the opinions of mankind, and whether the opinion maintained a decent respect for us, or whether like Athens of old, we will forfeit sympathy and support, and ultimately our very security, in a single-minded pursuit of our own goals and our own objectives.

SHIRLEY CHISHOLM

In 1968, Shirley Chisholm was the first African American woman elected to the U. S. House of Representatives. Protests were common during that time – especially regarding the Vietnam war, civil rights and women's rights – and Rep. Chisholm spoke out on all of those issues. In a statement to Congress in 1969, she introduced the Equal Rights Amendment. Women were asking for access to the same opportunities as men, especially in the areas of finances, education, and employment. This amendment, which had been introduced to every Congress since 1923, stated "Equality of rights under the law shall not be denied or abridged by the United States or by any State on account of sex." Congress finally passed the Amendment in 1972 and sent it to the states. It died in 1982, being three states short of ratification.

"EQUAL RIGHTS FOR WOMEN" ADDRESS TO THE U.S. HOUSE OF REPRESENTATIVES MAY 21, 1969

Mr. Speaker, when a young woman graduates from college and starts looking for a job, she is likely to have a frustrating and even demeaning experience ahead of her. If she walks into an office for an interview, the first question she will be asked is, "Do you type?"

There is a calculated system of prejudice that lies unspoken behind that question. Why is it acceptable for women to be secretaries, librarians, and teachers, but totally unacceptable for them to be managers, administrators, doctors, lawyers, and Members of Congress. The unspoken assumption is that women are different. They do not have executive ability, orderly minds, stability, leadership skills, and they are too emotional.

It has been observed before, that society for a long time, discriminated against another minority, the blacks, on the same basis – that they were different and inferior. The happy little homemaker and the contented "old darkey" on the plantation were both produced by prejudice.

As a black person, I am no stranger to race prejudice. But the truth is that in the political world I have been far oftener discriminated against because I am a woman than because I am black.

Prejudice against blacks is becoming unacceptable although it will take years to eliminate it. But it is doomed because, slowly, white America is beginning to admit that it exists. Prejudice against women is still acceptable. There is very little understanding yet of the immorality involved in double pay scales and the classification of most of the better jobs as "for men only."

More than half of the population of the United States is female. But women occupy only 2 percent of the managerial positions. They have not even reached the level of tokenism yet. No women sit on the AFL-CIO council or Supreme Court. There have been only two women who have held Cabinet rank, and at present there are none. Only two women now hold ambassadorial rank in the diplomatic corps. In Congress, we are down to one Senator and ten Representatives.

Considering that there are about three and a half million more women in the United States than men, this situation is outrageous.

It is true that part of the problem has been that women have not been aggressive in demanding their rights. This was also true of the black population for many years. They submitted to oppression and even cooperated with it. Women have done the same thing. But now there is an awareness of this situation particularly among the younger segment of the population.

As in the field of equal rights for blacks, Spanish-Americans, the Indians, and other groups, laws will not change such deep-seated problems overnight. But they can be used to provide protection for those who are most abused, and to begin the process of evolutionary change by compelling the insensitive majority to reexamine its unconscious attitudes.

It is for this reason that I wish to introduce today a proposal that has been before every Congress for the last 40 years and that sooner or later must become part of the basic law of the land – the equal rights amendment.

Let me note and try to refute two of the commonest arguments that are offered against this amendment. One is that women are already protected under the law and do not need legislation. Existing laws are not adequate to secure equal rights for women. Sufficient proof of this is the concentration of women in lower paying, menial, unrewarding jobs and their incredible scarcity in the upper level jobs. If women are already equal, why is it such an event whenever one happens to be elected to Congress?

It is obvious that discrimination exists. Women do not have the opportunities that men do. And women that do not conform to the system, who try to break with the accepted patterns, are stigmatized as "odd" and "unfeminine." The fact is that a woman who aspires to be chairman of the board, or a Member of the House, does so for exactly the same reasons as any man. Basically, these are that she thinks she can do the job and she wants to try.

A second argument often heard against the equal rights amendment is that it would eliminate legislation that many States and the Federal Government have enacted giving special protection to women and that it would throw the marriage and divorce laws into chaos.

As for the marriage laws, they are due for a sweeping reform, and an excellent beginning would be to wipe the existing ones off the books. Regarding special protection for working women, I cannot understand why it should be needed. Women need no protection that men do not need. What we need are laws to protect working people, to guarantee them fair pay, safe working conditions, protection against sickness and layoffs, and provision for dignified, comfortable retirement. Men and women need these things equally. That one sex needs protection more than the other is a male supremacist myth as ridiculous and unworthy of respect as the white supremacist myths that society is trying to cure itself of at this time.

Elizabeth Glaser

Elizabeth Glaser was infected with HIV through a transfusion and before the disease was diagnosed, passed it on to her two children. She co-founded the Pediatric AIDS Foundation to raise money for research and education. She also wrote her autobiography, In the Absence of Angels, *in which she described her efforts to learn about pediatric AIDS and bring the problem to the attention of congressional leaders. In 1994, at the age of 47, she died of AIDS-related complications.*

Address to the Democratic National Convention July 14, 1992

I'm Elizabeth Glaser. Eleven years ago, while giving birth to my first child, I hemorrhaged and was transfused with seven pints of blood. Four years later, I found out that I had been infected with the AIDS virus and had unknowingly passed it on to my daughter, Ariel, through my breast milk, and my son, Jake, in utero.

Twenty years ago I wanted to be at the Democratic Convention because it was a way to participate in our country. Today I am here because it's a matter of life and death. Exactly four years ago my daughter died of AIDS – she did not survive the Reagan administration. I am here because my son and I may not survive four more years of leaders who say they care, but do nothing. I am in a race with the clock. This is not about being a Republican or an Independent or a Democrat – it's about the future…for each and every one of us.

I started out just a mom – fighting for the life of her child. But along the way I learned how unfair America can be. Not just for the people who have HIV, but for many, many people – gay people, people of color, children. A strange spokesperson for such a group – a well-to-do white woman – but I have learned my lessons the hard way, and I know that America has lost her path and is at risk of losing her soul. America wake up – we are all in a struggle between life and death.

I understand the sense of frustration and despair in our country, because I know firsthand about screaming for help and getting no answer. I went to Washington to tell Presidents Reagan and Bush we needed to do much, much more for AIDS research and care, and that children couldn't be forgotten. The first time, when nothing happened, I thought, oh, they just didn't hear. The second time, when nothing happened, I thought, maybe I didn't shout loud enough. But now I realize that they don't hear because they don't want to listen. When you cry for help and no one listens, you start to lose hope.

I began to lose faith in America. I felt my own country was letting me down – and it was. This is not the America I was raised to be proud of. I was raised to believe that other's problems were my problems as well. But when I tell most people about HIV, hoping they will care and try to help, I see the look in their eyes – it's not my problem they're thinking – well, it's everyone's problem and we need a leader who will tell us that.

We need a visionary to guide us – to say it wasn't all right for Ryan White to be banned from school because he had HIV or a man or woman denied a job because they were infected with this virus. We need a leader who is truly committed to educating us.

I believe in America – but not with a leadership of selfishness and greed where the wealthy get health care and insurance and the poor don't. Do you know how much my AIDS care costs? More than $40,000 a year. Someone without insurance can't afford this. Even the drugs that I hope will keep me alive are out of reach for others. Is their life any less valuable? Of course not. This is not the America I was raised to be proud of – where the rich people get care and drugs that poor people can't. We need health care for all. We need a leader to say this, and do something about it.

I believe in America, but not with a leadership that talks about problems but is incapable of solving them. Two HIV commission reports with recommendations about what to do to solve this crisis are sitting on shelves, gathering dust. We need a leader who will not only listen to these recommendations, but will implement them.

I believe in America – but not with a leadership that doesn't hold government accountable. I go to Washington to the National Institutes of Health and say, "Show me what you're doing on HIV." They hate it when I come because I try to tell them how to do it better. But that's why I love being a taxpayer – because it's my money and they must become accountable.

I believe in an America where our leaders talk straight. When anyone tells President Bush that the battle against AIDS is seriously under-funded, he juggles the numbers to mislead the public into thinking we're spending twice as much as we really are. While they play games with numbers, people are dying.

I believe in America – but an America where there is light in every home. One thousand points of light just wasn't enough – my house has been dark for too long.

Once every generation, history brings us to an important crossroads. Sometimes in life there is that moment when it's possible to make a change for the better. This is one of those moments.

For me, this is not politics. It's a crisis of caring.

ALBERT GORE, JR.

Throughout his 24-year political career as a U. S. Congressman and Senator, then Vice President of the United States, Albert Gore has had an avid interest and abiding concern about global warming. He first learned of the climate crisis in the mid-sixties from Dr. Robert Revelle, one of his professors at Harvard University, who monitored levels of carbon dioxide in the Earth's atmosphere. As the years went by and CO_2 *concentration levels rose precipitously, Gore began to talk about the crisis and the need for new policies to reverse global warming. Congress resisted the changes for which he was calling, and President George H. W. Bush mockingly called him "Ozone Man." After winning the popular vote in the 2000 presidential election, but losing in the Electoral College, Gore focused his energies on global warming, presenting his slide show all around the world. The slide show evolved into an Oscar-winning documentary film. Together with the United Nations' Intergovernmental Panel on Climate Change, in 2007 Gore was awarded the Nobel Peace Prize.*

FROM HIS REMARKS AT GLACIER NATIONAL PARK SEPTEMBER 2, 1997

I thank all of you for joining me here in Glacier National Park – one of the greatest glories of America's park system. The rich landscape we see all around us – the deep valleys and dramatic summits – date back more than a billion years, when Ice Age glaciers cut through this terrain, shaping and sculpting what is now one of the largest wild areas in the United States.

The Blackfeet Indians called this land "the Backbone of the World" – and there is no question that, for the two million people who visit this park each year, Glacier connects us to the very core of our nature. It's a place where stunning summits overlook a million acres of wilderness; where the most rugged rock formations rub against meadows of beargrass blossoms; where grizzly bear, and elk, and bighorn sheep roam free.

It's easy to understand why Glacier means so much to the families that come here. It is a land that seems almost untouched by time, undamaged by man's heavy hand. To look out on Glacier's alpine beauty is to want to preserve it and protect it – for our children, and for our children's children.

I have come here today because Glacier National Park faces a grave threat to its heritage – and it's one that can't be met with a simple restoration plan. The 50 glaciers in this park – which date back to the last Ice Age, 10,000 years ago – are melting away at an alarming rate. Over the last century, we have lost nearly three-quarters of all the glaciers in this park. Grinnell Glacier has retreated by over 3,100 feet.

Jackson Glacier has lost about 75% of its surface area. If this trend continues, in about thirty years, there won't be any glaciers left at all. To borrow a phrase from a well-known pop musician, this could become be the Park Formerly Known as Glacier.

What's happening at Glacier National Park is strong evidence of global warming over the past century – the disruption of our climate because of greenhouse gas emissions into the atmosphere, all over the world. The overwhelming evidence shows that global warming is no longer a theory – it's a reality. Greenhouse gases keep rising at record rates. The last few decades have been the warmest of this century – and the ten warmest years in this century have all occurred since 1980.

My purpose today is not to be alarmist – nor is it to say that we need radical changes in the way we live and work. But it's time to face the facts: Global warming is *real.* We helped to cause it – and by taking reasonable, common-sense steps, we can help to reduce it.

What we need is an approach that is prudent and *balanced.* On one hand, we must recognize that energy consumption has led to enormous increases in our standard of living throughout this century, and we want to continue those increases. On the other hand, we see all around us today glaciers that have survived for 10,000 years, now facing the prospect of melting away in a single century. We've seen people struck by severe heat waves – more than 400 in Chicago just two years ago – and many others who have lost homes, jobs, even their lives to increasingly heavy storms.

We need to understand our role in climate change – and we need to act to address it.

As one ecologist recently told President Clinton and me at the White House, simply by *slowing* the rate of climate change, we can make it much easier for our environment to evolve and adapt to it.

But we know that America's efforts alone will never be good enough. Because winds circle the Earth within a few weeks, greenhouse gases don't respect national borders. Any real solution to global warming must be an *international* solution – including developing nations as well as industrialized ones.

This December, when the nations of the world meet in Kyoto, Japan on this issue, the United States will work to achieve realistic, binding limits on the emissions of greenhouse gases.

We will emphasize approaches that are flexible and market-based, to give industry the opportunity to develop the most cost-effective solutions.

We will continue our efforts in research and development. We will work with industry, with environmental groups, with *all* who share a stake in this problem here at home. And we will ask all nations, developed and developing, to join with us to meet this challenge.

We don't have all the answers today. But we know we must reverse the trend of global warming. We must safeguard our precious natural resources, and put a premium on public health and safety.

You see, thirty years from now, I want my grandchildren to live in a world that is safer from disease, freer from droughts and floods, able to grow the food they need for their children and families.

But just as importantly, I want them to understand that God created only one earth – and that its parks and forests and wilderness preserves can never be replicated. Our responsibility to this land is one of the most profound and sacred responsibilities we have. It is really a responsibility to each other – and to future generations.

Ultimately, that's why we came here today, to the very Crown of this Continent. We've got to start facing up to that responsibility – not just for the sake of these glaciers, but for the sake of our children. Here in the shadow of these glorious mountains, let us resolve to make that start – let us protect this land for its rightful inheritors – and let us fulfill our obligation to the millions of families who have yet to enjoy it.

ELIE WIESEL

At the age of 15, Elie Wiesel was deported with his family to Auschwitz where his mother and one of his sisters died. His father and he were later sent to Buchenwald, his father dying just before the camp was liberated in April 1945. After the war, Wiesel studied in Paris, became a journalist, and eventually began to write about his experiences in the death camps. In 1963, he became an American citizen and in 1978, President Carter appointed him chairman of the President's Commission on the Holocaust. He has received numerous awards and recognitions for his writing and human rights activities, including the 1986 Nobel Peace Prize. He currently works with the Elie Wiesel Foundation for Humanity, which he founded with his wife.

FROM "THE PERILS OF INDIFFERENCE"
MILLENNIUM LECTURE, THE WHITE HOUSE
APRIL 12, 1999

Fifty-four years ago to the day, a young Jewish boy from a small town in the Carpathian Mountains woke up, not far from Goethe's beloved Weimar, in a place of eternal infamy called Buchenwald. He was finally free, but there was no joy in his heart. He thought there never would be again. Liberated a day earlier by American soldiers, he remembers their rage at what they saw. And even if he lives to be a very old man, he will always be grateful to them for that rage, and also for their compassion. Though he did not understand their language, their eyes told him what he needed to know – that they, too, would remember, and bear witness.

We are on the threshold of a new century, a new millennium. What will the legacy of this vanishing century be? How will it be remembered in the new millennium? Surely it will be judged, and judged severely, in both moral and metaphysical terms. These failures have cast a dark shadow over humanity: two World Wars, countless civil wars, the senseless chain of assassinations – Gandhi, the Kennedys, Martin Luther King, Sadat, Rabin; bloodbaths in Cambodia and Nigeria, India and Pakistan, Ireland and Rwanda, Eritrea and Ethiopia, Sarajevo and Kosovo; the inhumanity in the gulag, and the tragedy of Hiroshima. And, on a different level, of course, Auschwitz and Treblinka. So much violence, so much indifference.

What is indifference? Etymologically, the word means "no difference." A strange and unnatural state in which the lines blur between light and darkness, dusk and dawn, crime and punishment, cruelty and compassion, good and evil. What are its courses and inescapable consequences? Is it a philosophy? Is there a philosophy of indifference conceivable? Can one possibly view indifference as a virtue? Is it necessary at times to practice it simply to keep one's sanity, live normally, enjoy a fine meal and a glass of wine, as the world around us experiences harrowing upheavals?

Of course, indifference can be tempting – more than that, seductive. It is so much easier to look away from victims. It is so much easier to avoid such rude interruptions to our work, our dreams, our hopes. It is, after all, awkward, troublesome, to be involved in another person's pain and despair. Yet, for the person who is indifferent, his or her neighbors are of no consequence. And, therefore, their lives are meaningless. Their hidden or even visible anguish is of no interest. Indifference reduces the other to an abstraction.

Over there, behind the black gates of Auschwitz, the most tragic of all prisoners were the "Muselmanner," as they were called. Wrapped in their torn blankets, they would sit or lie on the ground, staring vacantly into space, unaware of who or where they were, strangers to their surroundings. They no longer felt pain, hunger, thirst. They feared nothing. They felt nothing. They were dead and did not know it.

Rooted in our tradition, some of us felt that to be abandoned by humanity then was not the ultimate. We felt that to be abandoned by

God was worse than to be punished by Him. Better an unjust God than an indifferent one. For us to be ignored by God was a harsher punishment than to be a victim of His anger. Man can live far from God – not outside God. God is wherever we are. Even in suffering? Even in suffering.

In a way, to be indifferent to that suffering is what makes the human being inhuman. Indifference, after all, is more dangerous than anger and hatred. Anger can at times be creative. One writes a great poem, a great symphony. One does something special for the sake of humanity because one is angry at the injustice that one witnesses. But indifference is never creative. Even hatred at times may elicit a response. You fight it. You denounce it. You disarm it.

Indifference elicits no response. Indifference is not a response. Indifference is not a beginning, it is an end. And, therefore, indifference is always the friend of the enemy, for it benefits the aggressor – never his victim, whose pain is magnified when he or she feels forgotten. The political prisoner in his cell, the hungry children, the homeless refugees – not to respond to their plight, not to relieve their solitude by offering them a spark of hope is to exile them from human memory. And in denying their humanity we betray our own.

Indifference, then, is not only a sin, it is a punishment. And this is one of the most important lessons of this outgoing century's wide-ranging experiments in good and evil.

RUSSELL D. FEINGOLD

Six weeks after the September 11, 2001, attacks on the Pentagon and World Trade Center, Congress passed H.R. 3162 – the Uniting and Strengthening America By Providing Appropriate Tools Required to Intercept and Obstruct Terrorism Act of 2001. Commonly known as the U.S.A. Patriot Act, the bill had been rushed through the House and the Senate without committee hearings and with little debate. The purpose as cited in the Act was "to deter and punish terrorist acts in the United States and around the world, to enhance law enforcement investigating tools, and for other purposes." The vote in the U. S. Senate was 98-1. Russell Feingold, the only senator to vote against the bill, explained his position in a speech to the Senate from which the following excerpts are taken.

FROM HIS STATEMENT FROM THE FLOOR OF THE U. S. SENATE ON THE ANTI-TERRORISM BILL OCTOBER 25, 2001

I have approached the events of the past month and my role in proposing and reviewing legislation relating to it in this spirit.... We must redouble our vigilance to ensure our security and to prevent further acts of terror. But we must also redouble our vigilance to preserve our values and the basic rights that make us who we are.

The Founders who wrote our Constitution and Bill of Rights exercised that vigilance even though they had recently fought and won the Revolutionary War. They did not live in comfortable and easy times of hypothetical enemies. They wrote a Constitution of limited powers and an explicit Bill of Rights to protect liberty in times of war, as well as in times of peace.

There have been periods in our nation's history when civil liberties have taken a back seat to what appeared at the time to be the legitimate exigencies of war. Our national consciousness still bears the stain and the scars of those events: The Alien and Sedition Acts, the suspension of habeas corpus during the Civil War; the internment of Japanese-Americans, German-Americans, and Italian-Americans during World War II, the blacklisting of supposed communist sympathizers during the McCarthy era, and the surveillance and harassment of antiwar protesters, including Dr. Martin Luther King Jr., during the Vietnam War. We must not allow these pieces of our past to become prologue.

Mr. President, even in our great land, wartime has sometimes brought us the greatest tests of our Bill of Rights. For example, during the Civil War, the government arrested some 13,000 civilians, implementing a system akin to martial law. President Lincoln issued a proclamation ordering the arrest and military trial of any persons "discouraging volunteer enlistments, or resisting militia drafts." Wisconsin provided one of the first challenges of this order. Draft protests rose up in Milwaukee and Sheboygan. And an anti-draft riot broke out among Germans and Luxembourgers in Port Washington, Wisconsin. When the government arrested one of the leaders of the riot, his attorney sought a writ of habeas corpus. His military captors said that the President had abolished the writ. The Wisconsin Supreme Court was among the first to rule that the President had exceeded his authority.

In 1917, the Postmaster General revoked the mailing privileges of the newspaper the *Milwaukee Leader* because he felt that some of its articles impeded the war effort and the draft. Articles called the President an aristocrat and called the draft oppressive. Over dissents by Justices Brandeis and Holmes, the Supreme Court upheld the action.

During World War II, President Roosevelt signed orders to incarcerate more than 110,000 people of Japanese origin, as well as some roughly 11,000 of German origin and 3,000 of Italian origin. Earlier this year, I introduced legislation to set up a commission to review the wartime treatment of Germans, Italians, and other Europeans during that period. That bill came out of heartfelt meetings in which constituents told me their stories. They were German-Americans, who came to me with some trepidation. They had waited 50 years to raise the issue with a member of Congress. They did not want compensation. But they had seen the government's commission on the wartime internment of people of Japanese origin, and they wanted their story to be told, and an official acknowledgment as well. I hope, Mr. President, that we will move to pass this important legislation early next year. We must deal with our nation's past, even as we move to ensure our nation's future.

Now some may say, indeed we may hope, that we have come a long way since those days of infringements on civil liberties. But there is ample reason for concern. And I have been troubled in the past six weeks by the potential loss of commitment in the Congress and the country to traditional civil liberties.

As it seeks to combat terrorism, the Justice Department is making extraordinary use of its power to arrest and detain individuals, jailing hundreds of people on immigration violations and arresting more than a dozen "material witnesses" not charged with any crime. Although the government has used these authorities before, it has not done so on such a broad scale. Judging from government announcements, the government has not brought any criminal charges related to the attacks with regard to the overwhelming majority of these detainees....

Even as America addresses the demanding security challenges before us, we must strive mightily also to guard our values and basic rights. We must guard against racism and ethnic discrimination against people of Arab and South Asian origin and those who are Muslim.

We who don't have Arabic names or don't wear turbans or headscarves may not feel the weight of these times as much as Americans from the Middle East and South Asia do. But as the great jurist Learned Hand said in a speech in New York's Central Park during World War II: "The spirit of liberty is the spirit which seeks to understand the minds of other men and women; the spirit of liberty is the spirit which weighs their interests alongside its own without bias."...

Of course, given the enormous anxiety and fears generated by the events of September 11th, it would not have been difficult to anticipate some of these reactions, both by our government and some of our people. Some have said rather cavalierly that in these difficult times we must accept some reduction in our civil liberties in order to be secure.

Of course, there is no doubt that if we lived in a police state, it would be easier to catch terrorists. If we lived in a country that allowed the police to search your home at any time for any reason; if we lived in a country that allowed the government to open your mail, eavesdrop on your phone conversations, or intercept your email communications; if we lived in a country that allowed the government to hold people in jail indefinitely based on what they write or think, or based on mere suspicion that they are up to no good, then the government would no doubt discover and arrest more terrorists.

But that probably would not be a country in which we would want to live. And that would not be a country for which we could, in good conscience, ask our young people to fight and die. In short, that would not be America.

Preserving our freedom is one of the main reasons that we are now engaged in this new war on terrorism. We will lose that war without firing a shot if we sacrifice the liberties of the American people.

BARACK OBAMA

Born in Hawaii, the son of a Kenyan and a Kansan, Barack Obama was raised in Honolulu and Jakarta. He graduated from Columbia University and Harvard Law School, and worked in Chicago as a community organizer and civil rights lawyer. Obama came to national attention when he gave the keynote address at the 2004 Democratic National Convention. At that time, he had been an Illinois State Senator for eight years, and was running for a seat in the U. S. Senate, which he subsequently won. In both of these elected offices, he helped pass bills on ethics and lobbying reform, which he speaks about in the following remarks.

FROM HIS OPENING STATEMENT FROM THE FLOOR OF THE U. S. SENATE ON ETHICS REFORM MARCH 7, 2006

Over one hundred years ago, at the dawn of the last century, the Industrial Revolution was beginning to take hold of America, creating unimaginable wealth in sprawling metropolises all across the country. As factories multiplied and profits grew, the winnings of the new economy became more and more concentrated in the hands of a few robber barons, railroad tycoons and oil magnates. In the cities, power was maintained by a corrupt system of political machines and ward bosses. And in the state of New York, there was a young governor who was determined to give government back to the people.

In just his first year, he had already begun to antagonize the state's political machine by attacking its system of favors and corporate giveaways. He also signed a workers' compensation bill, and even fired the superintendent of insurance for taking money from the very industry he was supposed to be regulating.

None of this sat too well with New York's powerful party boss, who finally plotted to get rid of the reform-minded governor by making sure he was nominated for the Vice Presidency that year. What no one could have expected is that soon after the election, when President William McKinley was assassinated, the greatest fears of the corrupt machine bosses and powerbrokers came true when that former governor became President of the United States and went on to bust trusts, break up monopolies, and return the government to its people.

His name, of course, was Theodore Roosevelt. He was a Republican. And throughout his public life, he demonstrated a willingness to put party and politics aside in order to battle corruption and give people an open, honest government that would fight for their interests and uphold their values.

Today, we face a similar crisis of corruption. And I believe that we need similar leadership from those in power as well. The American people are tired of a Washington that's only open to those with the most cash and the right connections. They're tired of a political process where the vote you cast isn't as important as the favors you can do. And they're tired of trusting us with their tax dollars when they see them spent on frivolous pet projects and corporate giveaways.

It's not that the games that are played in this town are new or surprising to the public. People are not naive to the existence of corruption and they know it has worn the face of both Republicans and Democrats over the years. Moreover, the underlying issue of how extensively money influences politics is the original sin of everyone who's ever run for office – myself included. In order to get elected, we need to raise vast sums of money by meeting and dealing with people who are disproportionately wealthy....

Yet, while people know that both parties are vulnerable to these problems, I do think it's fair to say that the scandals we've seen under the current White House and Congress – both legal and illegal – are far worse than most of us could have imagined.

Think about it. In the past several months, we've seen the head of the White House procurement office arrested. We've seen some of our most powerful leaders of both the House and the Senate under federal investigation. We've seen the indictment of Jack Abramoff and his cronies. And of course, last week, we saw a member of Congress sentenced to eight years in prison for bribery.

Now, some have dismissed these scandals by saying that "everybody does it." Well, not everybody does it. And people shouldn't lump together those of us who have to raise funds to run campaigns but do so in a legal and ethical way with those who invite lobbyists in to write bad legislation. Those aren't equivalent, and we're not being partisan by pointing that out....

What's truly offensive about these scandals is that they don't just lead to morally offensive conduct on the part of politicians; they lead to morally offensive legislation that hurts hardworking Americans.

When big oil companies are invited into the White House for secret energy meetings, it's no wonder they end up with billions in tax breaks while most working people struggle to fill up their gas tanks and heat their homes.

When a Committee Chairman negotiates a Medicare bill one day and then negotiates for a job with the drug industry the next, it's hardly a surprise that that industry gets taxpayer-funded giveaways in the same bill that forbids seniors from bargaining for better drug prices.

When the people running Washington are accountable only to the special interests that fund their campaigns, it's not shocking that the American people find their tax dollars being spent with reckless abandon.

Since George Bush took office, we've seen the number of registered lobbyists in Washington double. In 2004, over $2.1 billion was spent lobbying Congress. That amounts to over $4.8 million per Member of Congress.

How much do you think the American people were able to spend on their Senators or Representatives last year? How much money could the folks who can't fill up their gas tanks spend? How much could the seniors forced to choose between their medications and their groceries spend?

Not $4.8 million. Not even close.

This is the bigger story here. The American people believe that the well-connected CEOs and hired guns on K Street who've helped write our laws have gotten what they paid for. They got all the tax breaks and loopholes and access they could ever want. But outside this city, the people who can't afford the high-priced lobbyists and don't want to break the law are wondering, "When is it our turn? When will someone in Washington stand up for me?"

We need to answer that call. Because while only some are to blame for the corruption that has plagued this city, all are responsible for fixing it....

But to truly earn back the people's trust - to show them that we're working for them and looking out for their interests – we have to do more than just pass a good bill this week. We have to fundamentally change the way we do business around here.

That means instead of meeting with lobbyists, it's time to start meeting with some of the 45 million Americans with no health care.

Instead of finding cushy political jobs for unqualified buddies, it's time to start finding good-paying jobs for hardworking Americans trying to raise a family.

Instead of hitting up the big firms on K Street, it's time to start visiting the workers on Main Street who wonder how they'll send their kids to college or whether their pension will be around when they retire.

All these people have done to earn access and gain influence is cast their ballot. But in this democracy, it's all anyone should have to do.

A century ago, that young, reform-minded governor of New York who later became our twenty-sixth President gave us words about our country everyone in this town would do well to listen to today. Teddy Roosevelt said that,

> *No republic can permanently endure when its politics are corrupt and base...we can afford to differ on the currency, the tariff, and foreign policy, but we cannot afford to differ on the question of honesty. There is a soul in the community, a soul in the nation, just exactly as there is a soul in the individual; and exactly as the individual hopelessly mars himself if he lets his conscience be dulled by the constant repetition of unworthy acts, so the nation will hopelessly blunt the popular conscience if it permits its public men continually to do acts which the nation in its heart of hearts knows are acts which cast discredit upon our whole public life.*

I hope that this week, we in the Senate will take the first step towards strengthening this nation's soul and bringing credit back to our public life.

JOHN F. KERRY

After graduating from Yale University in 1966, John Kerry became a naval officer, serving in Vietnam and receiving the Silver Star, the Bronze Star with combat V, and three Purple Hearts. He became disillusioned with the war and requested his discharge from the Navy in January 1970. Five months later, he joined Vietnam Veterans Against the War, becoming an unofficial spokesperson. In April 1971, Kerry helped organize a VVAW anti-war protest held on the Mall in Washington, D. C. For this and his outspoken efforts on behalf of VVAW, he was placed on President Richard Nixon's infamous "enemies list." During the protest, Kerry was asked to testify before the Senate Committee on Foreign Relations. On the 35th anniversary of this testimony, U. S. Senator Kerry gave the following address at historic Faneuil Hall in Boston.

A RIGHT AND RESPONSIBILITY TO SPEAK OUT
APRIL 22, 2006

Thirty-five years ago today, I testified before the Foreign Relations Committee of the United States Senate, and called for an end to the war I had returned from fighting not long before.

It was 1971 – twelve years after the first American died in what was then South Vietnam, seven years after Lyndon Johnson seized on a small and contrived incident in the Tonkin Gulf to launch a full-scale war – and three years after Richard Nixon was elected president on the promise of a secret plan for peace. We didn't know it at the time, but four more years of the War in Vietnam still lay ahead. These were years in which the Nixon administration lied and broke the law – and claimed it was prolonging war to protect our troops as they withdrew – years that ultimately ended only when politicians in Washington decided they would settle for a "decent interval" between the departure of our forces and the inevitable fall of Saigon.

I know that some active duty service members, some veterans, and certainly some politicians scorned those of us who spoke out, suggesting our actions failed to "support the troops" – which to them meant continuing to support the war, or at least keeping our mouths shut. Indeed, some of those critics said the same thing just two years ago during the presidential campaign.

I have come here today to reaffirm that it was right to dissent in 1971 from a war that was wrong. And to affirm that it is both a right and an obligation for Americans today to disagree with a President who is wrong, a policy that is wrong, and a war in Iraq that weakens the nation....

This is not the first time in American history when patriotism has been distorted to deflect criticism and mislead the nation.

In the infancy of the Republic, in 1798, Congress enacted the Alien and Sedition Acts to smear Thomas Jefferson and accuse him of treason. Newspapers were shut down, and their editors arrested, including Benjamin Franklin's grandson. No wonder Thomas Jefferson himself said: "Dissent is the greatest form of patriotism."

In the Mexican War, a young Congressman named Abraham Lincoln was driven from public life for raising doubts about official claims. And in World War I, America's values were degraded, not defended, when dissenters were jailed and the teaching of German was banned in public schools in some states. At that time it was apparently sounding German, not looking French, that got you in trouble. And it was panic and prejudice, not true patriotism, that brought the internment of Japanese-Americans during World War II – a measure upheld by Supreme Court Justices who did not uphold their oaths to defend the Constitution. We are stronger today because no less a rock-ribbed conservative than Robert Taft – "Mr. Republican" himself – stood up and said at the height of the second World War that, "the maintenance of the right of criticism in the long run will do the country maintaining it a great deal more good than it will do the enemy, and will prevent mistakes which might otherwise occur."

Even during the Cold War – an undeclared war, and often more a war of nerves and diplomacy than of arms – even the mildest dissenters from official policy were sometimes silenced, blacklisted, or arrested, especially during the McCarthy era of the early 1950s. Indeed, it was only when Joseph McCarthy went through the gates of delirium and began accusing distinguished U.S. diplomats and military leaders of treason that the two parties in Washington and the news media realized the common stake they had in the right to dissent. They stood up to a bully and brought down McCarthyism's ugly and contrived appeals to a phony form of 100% Americanism.

Dissenters are not always right, but it is always a warning sign when they are accused of unpatriotic sentiments by politicians seeking a safe harbor from debate, from accountability, or from the simple truth.

Truth is the American bottom line. Truth above all is fundamental to who we are. It is no accident that among the first words of the first declaration of our national existence it is proclaimed: "We hold these truths to be self-evident"...

And here and now we must insist again that fidelity, honor, and love of country demand untrammeled debate and open dissent. At no time is that truer than in the midst of a war rooted in deceit and justified by continuing deception. For what is at stake here is nothing less than life itself. As the statesman Edmund Burke once said: "A conscientious man should be cautious how he dealt in blood."

Think about that now – in a new era that has brought old temptations and tested abiding principles.

America has always embraced the best traditions of civilized conduct toward combatants and non-combatants in war. But today our leaders hold themselves above the law – in the way they not only treat prisoners in Abu Ghraib, but assert unchecked power to spy on American citizens.

America has always rejected war as an instrument of raw power or naked self-interest. We fought when we had to in order to repel grave threats or advance freedom and self-determination in concert with like-minded people everywhere. But our current leadership, for all its rhetoric of freedom and democracy, behaves as though might does make right, enabling us to discard the alliances and institutions that served us so well in the past as nothing more now than impediments to the exercise of unilateral power.

America has always been stronger when we have not only proclaimed free speech, but listened to it. Yes, in every war, there have been those who demand suppression and silencing. And although no one is being jailed today for speaking out against the war in Iraq, the spirit of intolerance for dissent has risen steadily, and the habit of labeling dissenters as unpatriotic has become the common currency of the politicians currently running our country.

Dismissing dissent is not only wrong, but dangerous when America's leadership is unwilling to admit mistakes, unwilling to engage in honest discussion of the nation's direction, and unwilling to hold itself accountable for the consequences of decisions made without genuine disclosure, or genuine debate....

I understand fully that Iraq is not Vietnam, and the war on terrorism is not the Cold War. But in one very crucial respect, we are in the same place now as we were thirty five years ago. When I testified in 1971, I spoke out not just against the war itself, but the blindness and cynicism of political leaders who were sending brave young Americans to be killed or maimed for a mission the leaders themselves no longer believed in.

The War in Vietnam and the War in Iraq are now converging in too many tragic respects.

As in Vietnam, we engaged militarily in Iraq based on official deception.

As in Vietnam, we went into Iraq ostensibly to fight a larger global war under the misperception that the particular theater was just a sideshow, but we soon learned that the particular aspects of the place where we fought mattered more than anything else.

And as in Vietnam, we have stayed and fought and died even though it is time for us to go....

So now, as in 1971, we are engaged in another fight to live the truth and make our own government accountable. As in 1971, this is another moment when American patriotism demands more dissent and less complacency in the face of bland assurances from those in power.

We must insist now that patriotism does not belong to those who defend a President's position – it belongs to those who defend their country. Patriotism is not love of power; it is love of country. And sometimes loving your country demands you must tell the truth to power. This is one of those times.

Lives are on the line. Lives have been lost to bad decisions – not decisions that could have gone either way, but decisions that constitute basic negligence and incompetence. And lives continue to be lost because of stubbornness and pride.

We support the troops – the brave men and women who have always protected us and do so today – in part by honoring their service, and in part by making sure they have everything they need both in battle and after they have borne the burden of battle.

But I believe now as strongly and proudly as I did thirty-five years ago that the most important way to support the troops is to tell the truth, and to ensure we do not ask young Americans to die in a cause that falls short of the ideals of this country.

When we protested the war in Vietnam some would weigh in against us saying: "My country right or wrong." Our response was simple: "Yes, my country right or wrong. When right, keep it right and when wrong, make it right." And that's what we must do again today.

JOHN LEWIS

Born in Alabama in 1940, John Lewis was the son of sharecroppers. By the age of 23, he was a nationally known leader of the Civil Rights Movement. A few of Lewis' activities in the early to mid-1960's included participating in the Freedom Rides to integrate interstate bus travel, helping to form and serving as chairman of the Student Nonviolent Coordinating Committee, organizing and being a keynote speaker at the 1963 March on Washington, and leading the march for voting rights in 1965 in Selma, Alabama, which ended shortly after it began when state troopers attacked the marchers at the Edmund Pettus Bridge. Countless beatings and arrests did not deter him. He was elected to the U.S. House of Representatives from Georgia's 5th District in 1986, an office he continues to hold. In 2001, he was awarded the first Profiles in Courage Lifetime Achievement Award.

"DEPARTMENT OF PEACE" - EXTENSIONS OF HIS REMARKS IN THE U. S. HOUSE OF REPRESENTATIVES FEBRUARY 7, 2007

Madam Speaker, I rise today to support the establishment of a Department of Peace and Nonviolence as a cabinet-level office of the executive branch of our government. I agree with Representative Kucinich that war and the threat of war have dominated international relationships for much too long. As a participant in the Civil Rights Movement, as a human being who has faced the barrel of a loaded gun armed only with the philosophy of peace, it has been my belief for many years that war is obsolete as a tool of our foreign policy. But I realize that position may be too progressive for many of my colleagues to accept.

But maybe, just maybe at this moment in our nation's history, when we find ourselves struggling with the hopeless legacy of violence, maybe, just maybe we might be willing to consider the methods of peace as an intelligent, strategic alternative to war. At this very moment our sons and daughters are battling in the middle of an unnecessary war, a war we started, hoping that we could force democracy to grow.

But Mahatma Gandhi once said that violence begets violence. And a recipient of the Nobel Prize for Peace, Martin Luther King, Jr., once said if we as a people want peaceful ends, we must use peaceful means. When will the warring factions in Syria, Lebanon, Israel, Iran, Iraq, Afghanistan and the United States be willing to say they have spilled enough innocent blood? When will they say it is time for us to lay down the tools and instruments of war? Today, can we hear the words of Gandhi, perhaps stronger now than ever before, "We must choose non-violence or non-existence?"

Are we finally willing to hear the words of Martin Luther King, Jr., "We must learn to live as brothers and sisters or perish as fools?" Can we, the most powerful nation in the world, use our influence, to raise these questions and give peace a chance?

Madam Speaker, as a nation and as a people we have researched, written about, studied, constructed, deployed and spent trillions of dollars on the best ways to destroy humanity. We have used the power of fear to dominate world affairs. What would happen if the most powerful nation on earth took the lead and through this Department of Peace decided to put even half of those resources toward developing ways to sustain humanity, ways to keep the peace in spite of competing international interests, and ways to gain influence using the power of diplomacy and negotiation?

Without constructive, alternative policies, without viable tools that leaders of nations and leaders of human kind can reach for, peace will always be a vanishing ideal that holds no substance. If we truly believe that peace is our ultimate goal, then we must use the resources of this great nation to that end. We must use the brilliance of American intelligence to develop the methods and mechanisms of peace, even more actively than we develop the mechanisms of war. That's why we need a Peace Academy that will create a diplomatic corps armed with the tools of peaceful influence.

We are all one people, Madam Speaker. We are one family, the human family, and we must find a way to understand each other, to make peace, and learn to live together.

PRINCIPLES

THE ESSENTIAL PRINCIPLES OF OUR GOVERNMENT FORM THE BRIGHT CONSTELLATION WHICH HAS GONE BEFORE US AND GUIDED OUR STEPS THROUGH AN AGE OF REVOLUTION AND REFORMATION. THE WISDOM OF OUR SAGES AND BLOOD OF OUR HEROES HAVE BEEN DEVOTED TO THEIR ATTAINMENT. THEY SHOULD BE THE CREED OF OUR POLITICAL FAITH, THE TEXT OF CIVIC INSTRUCTION, THE TOUCHSTONE BY WHICH TO TRY THE SERVICES OF THOSE WE TRUST; AND SHOULD WE WANDER FROM THEM IN MOMENTS OF ERROR OR OF ALARM, LET US HASTEN TO RETRACE OUR STEPS AND TO REGAIN THE ROAD WHICH ALONE LEADS TO PEACE, LIBERTY AND SAFETY.

Thomas Jefferson
First Inaugural Address
Washington, D.C.
March 4, 1801

THOMAS JEFFERSON

Thomas Jefferson was first and foremost a farmer, whose vision for the United States was that of an agricultural society made up of family farms served by local community businesses. These communities would be democratically governed by well-educated citizens who were guaranteed freedom of thought and freedom to speak openly about those thoughts. Jefferson feared the strong national government favored by Alexander Hamilton, with its focus on manufacturing and businesses run by a privileged aristocracy, would soon become a monarchical society limiting the freedoms of the common citizen. This polarity led to the formation of the nation's first political parties, the Federalist Party led by Hamilton and the Democratic-Republican Party led by Jefferson.

FROM HIS LETTER TO HENRY LEE 1824

Men by their constitutions are naturally divided into two parties: 1. Those who fear and distrust the people, and wish to draw all powers from them into the hands of the higher classes. 2. Those who identify themselves with the people, have confidence in them, cherish and consider them as the most honest and safe, although not the most wise depositary of the public interests. In every country these two parties exist, and in every one where they are free to think, speak, and write, they will declare themselves. Call them, therefore, Liberals and Serviles, Jacobins and Ultras, Whigs and Tories, Republicans and Federalists, Aristocrats and Democrats, or by whatever name you please, they are the same parties still and pursue the same object. The last one of Aristocrats and Democrats is the true one expressing the essence of all.

ANDREW JACKSON

A popular war hero, Andrew Jackson ran for president in 1824. He lost to John Quincy Adams in the House of Representatives even though he had won a plurality of both the popular and electoral college votes. In protest, a coalition of Jackson supporters who thought Adams had stolen the election and "Radicals" who were opposed to a strong national government split from the Democratic-Republican Party to form the Democratic Party. Jackson won the presidency in 1828, having urged voters to "vote for us if you believe the people should govern."

Seeking a political advantage a few months prior to the 1832 election, Jackson's opponents pushed through Congress a bill re-chartering the Second Bank of the United States. The charter of the bank, a private corporation which held the gold and silver assets of the U. S. government, was due to expire in 1836. Jackson believed the Bank to be unconstitutional, to favor the wealthy, and to be unfairly contributing money to political candidates and newspapers who supported the Bank. He promptly vetoed the bill and the Bank became a major issue in that year's campaign. Jackson went on to win the election and ultimately withdrew the government's money from the Bank.

FROM HIS FIRST ANNUAL MESSAGE TO CONGRESS
December 4, 1829

Our government springs from and was made for the people – not the people for the government. To them it owes allegiance; from them it must derive its courage, strength, and wisdom.

FROM HIS BANK VETO MESSAGE JULY 10, 1832

It is to be regretted that the rich and powerful too often bend the acts of government to their selfish purposes. Distinctions in society will always exist under every just government. Equality of talents, of education, or of wealth cannot be produced by human institutions. In the full enjoyment of the gifts of Heaven and the fruits of superior industry, economy, and virtue, every man is equally entitled to protection by law; but when the laws undertake to add to these natural and just advantages artificial distinctions, to grant titles, gratuities, and exclusive privileges, to make the rich richer and the potent more powerful, the humble members of society, the farmers, mechanics, and laborers who have neither the time nor the means of securing like favors to themselves, have a right to complain of the injustice of their Government. There are no necessary evils in government. Its evils exist only in its abuses. If it would confine itself to equal protection, and as Heaven does its rains, shower its favors alike on the high and the low, the rich and the poor, it would be an unqualified blessing.

FRANKLIN D. ROOSEVELT

Due to his duties as commander in chief during World War II and his poor health, Franklin Roosevelt did not begin his re-election campaign for his fourth term until he gave this speech to the Teamsters' Union in Washington, D.C. It is known as the Fala Speech because toward the end of the text, Roosevelt responds to unsubstantiated Republican charges that he sent a destroyer back to the Aleutian Islands where he had inadvertently left his dog Fala, costing the taxpayers millions of dollars. Roosevelt handily defeated Thomas Dewey but died less than six weeks after beginning his fourth term in office.

FROM HIS ADDRESS TO THE INTERNATIONAL BROTHERHOOD OF TEAMSTERS, CHAUFFEURS, WAREHOUSEMEN, AND HELPERS OF AMERICA, SEPTEMBER 23, 1944

We all know that certain people who make it a practice to depreciate the accomplishments of labor – who even attack labor as unpatriotic – they keep this up usually for three years and six months in a row. But then, for some strange reason they change their tune – every four years – just before election day. When votes are at stake, they suddenly discover that they really love labor and that they are anxious to protect labor from its old friends.

I got quite a laugh, for example – and I am sure that you did – when I read this plank in the Republican platform adopted at their National Convention in Chicago last July: "The Republican Party accepts the purposes of the National Labor Relations Act, the Wage and Hour Act, the Social Security Act and all other Federal statutes designed to promote and protect the welfare of American working men and women, and we promise a fair and just administration of these laws."

You know, many of the Republican leaders and Congressmen and candidates, who shouted enthusiastic approval of that plank in that Convention Hall would not even recognize these progressive laws if they met them in broad daylight. Indeed, they have personally spent years of effort and energy – and much money – in fighting every one of those laws in the Congress, and in the press, and in the courts, ever since this Administration began to advocate them and enact them into legislation. That is a fair example of their insincerity and of their inconsistency.

The whole purpose of Republican oratory these days seems to be to switch labels. The object is to persuade the American people that the Democratic Party was responsible for the 1929 crash and the depression, and that the Republican Party was responsible for all social progress under the New Deal.

Now, imitation may be the sincerest form of flattery – but I am afraid that in this case it is the most obvious common or garden variety of fraud.

Of course, it is perfectly true that there are enlightened, liberal elements in the Republican Party, and they have fought hard and honorably to bring the party up to date and to get it in step with the forward march of American progress. But these liberal elements were not able to drive the Old Guard Republicans from their entrenched positions.

Can the Old Guard pass itself off as the New Deal? I think not.

HARRY S. TRUMAN

During the presidential election campaign of 1948, the Democratic Party splintered into three factions. The party's candidate was Harry Truman, who had become President in April 1945 upon the death of Franklin Roosevelt. Southern Democrats (also known as Dixiecrats), who disagreed with Truman's strong support of civil rights for blacks, formed a States Rights Party whose nominee was Strom Thurmond. Liberals broke from the Democratic Party and nominated Henry Wallace as the candidate of the new Progressive Party. The Republican Party's candidate was once again Thomas Dewey, who looked like a sure winner against the unpopular president and the fractured Democrats. However, Truman took his campaign on a series of three whistle-stop campaign trips, where he spoke to the people from the back of the train. Surprising just about everyone, including the editors of newspapers with headlines declaring Dewey the winner, Truman won the election handily.

WHISTLE-STOP CAMPAIGN SPEECH
ELIZABETH, NEW JERSEY
OCTOBER 7, 1948

You are here because you are interested in the issues of this campaign. You know, as all the citizens of this great country know, that the election is not all over nothing but shouting. That is what they would like to have you believe, but it isn't so – it isn't so at all.

The Republicans are trying to hide the truth from you in a great many ways. They don't want you to know the truth about the issues in this campaign. The big fundamental issue in this campaign is the people against the special interests.

The Democratic Party stands for the people.

The Republican Party stands, and always has stood, for special interests. They have proved that conclusively in the record that they made in this "do-nothing" Congress.

The Republican Party candidates are going around talking to you in high-sounding platitudes, trying to make you believe that they themselves are the best people to run the government. Well now, you have had experience with them running the government. In 1920 to 1932, they had complete control of the government. Look what they did to it!...

This country is enjoying the greatest prosperity it has ever known because we have been following, for sixteen years, the policies inaugurated by Franklin D. Roosevelt. Everybody benefited from these policies – labor, the farmer, businessmen, and white-collar workers.

We want to keep that prosperity. We cannot keep that if we don't lick the biggest problem facing us today, and that is high prices.

I have been trying to get the Republicans to do something about high prices and housing ever since they came to Washington. They are responsible for that situation, because they killed price control, and they killed the housing bill. That Republican 80th "do-nothing" Congress absolutely refused to give any relief whatever in either one of those categories.

What do you suppose the Republicans think you ought to do about high prices? Senator Taft, one of the leaders in the Republican Congress, said, "If consumers think the price is too high today, they will wait until the price is lower. I feel that in time, the law of supply and demand will bring prices into line."

There is the Republican answer to the high cost of living. If it costs too much, just wait. If you think fifteen cents is too much for a loaf of bread, just do without it and wait until you can afford to pay fifteen cents for it. If you don't want to pay sixty cents a pound for hamburger, just wait. That is what the Republican Congress thought you ought to do, and that is the same Congress that the Republican candidate for president said did a good job.

Some people say I ought not to talk so much about the Republican 80th "do-nothing" Congress in this campaign. I will tell you why I will talk about it. If two-thirds of the people stay at home again on election day as they did in 1946, and if we get another Republican Congress like the 80th Congress, it will be controlled by the same men who controlled that 80th Congress – the Tabers and the Tafts, the Martins and the Hallecks would be the bosses. The same men would be the bosses, the same as those who passed the Taft-Hartley Act, and passed the rich man's tax bill, and took Social Security away from a million workers.

Do you want that kind of administration? I don't believe you do – I don't believe you do. I don't believe you would be out here, interested in listening to my outline of what the Republicans are trying to do to you, if you intended to put them back in there.

When a bunch of Republican reactionaries are in control of the Congress, then the people get reactionary laws. The only way you can get the kind of government you need is by going to the polls and voting the straight Democratic ticket on November 2. Then you will get a Democratic Congress, and I will get a Congress that will work with me. Then we will get good housing at prices we can afford to pay; and repeal of that vicious Taft-Hartley Act; and more Social Security coverage; and prices that will be fair to everybody; and we can go on and keep sixty-one million people at work; we can have an income of more than $217 billion, and that income will be distributed so that the farmer, the workingman, the white collar worker, and the businessman get their fair share of that income.

That is what I stand for. That is what the Democratic Party stands for. Vote for that, and you will be safe.

JOHN F. KENNEDY

John Kennedy believed that it was vitally important that his inaugural address set the tone for his administration. As examples of the type of speech he wanted to give, he looked to Franklin Roosevelt and Abraham Lincoln. Roosevelt, through his inspirational first inaugural address, sought to allay the fears of Americans about the Depression, and to instill hope of better days to come through a shared commitment to solve their problems. The oratorical eloquence of the Gettysburg Address was a result of Lincoln's brevity and simplicity. In his address, Kennedy stressed global issues and reiterated his campaign focus of national purpose and responsibility.

FROM HIS INAUGURAL ADDRESS
JANUARY 20, 1961

We observe today not a victory of party but a celebration of freedom – symbolizing an end as well as a beginning – signifying renewal as well as change. For I have sworn before you and Almighty God the same solemn oath our forebears prescribed nearly a century and three-quarters ago.

The world is very different now. For man holds in his mortal hands the power to abolish all forms of human poverty and all forms of human life. And yet the same revolutionary beliefs for which our forebears fought are still at issue around the globe – the belief that the rights of man come not from the generosity of the state but from the hand of God.

We dare not forget today that we are the heirs of that first revolution. Let the word go forth from this time and place, to friend and foe alike, that the torch has been passed to a new generation of Americans – born in this century, tempered by war, disciplined by a hard and bitter peace, proud of our ancient heritage – and unwilling to witness or permit the slow undoing of those human rights to which this nation has always been committed, and to which we are committed today at home and around the world.

Let every nation know, whether it wishes us well or ill, that we shall pay any price, bear any burden, meet any hardship, support any friend, oppose any foe to assure the survival and the success of liberty.

This much we pledge – and more.

In the long history of the world, only a few generations have been granted the role of defending freedom in its hour of maximum danger. I do not shrink from this responsibility – I welcome it. I do not believe that any of us would exchange places with any other people or any other generation. The energy, the faith, the devotion which we bring to this endeavor will light our country and all who serve it – and the glow from that fire can truly light the world....

And so, my fellow Americans: ask not what your country can do for you – ask what you can do for your country.

My fellow citizens of the world: ask not what America will do for you, but what together we can do for the freedom of man.

MARTIN LUTHER KING, JR.

In 1941, A. Philip Randolph, president of the Brotherhood of Sleeping Car Porters, proposed a march on Washington, D.C., by 100,000 African Americans. Although that march never materialized, President Franklin Roosevelt responded by creating the Fair Employment Practices Committee. Twenty-two years later, on August 28, 1963, Randolph and a coalition of five civil rights organizations led 250,000 peaceful and orderly demonstrators from the Washington Monument to the Lincoln Memorial in the March on Washington for Jobs and Freedom. The purpose of the march was to bring attention to the needs of African Americans in the areas of civil rights, desegregation, job training, and wage inequities. Once the marchers reached the Lincoln Memorial, they listened to a few musical performances and remarks by a wide range of well-known speakers, the last being Dr. Martin Luther King, who spoke of his dream for America.

FROM HIS "I HAVE A DREAM" ADDRESS DELIVERED AT THE MARCH ON WASHINGTON FOR JOBS AND FREEDOM AUGUST 28, 1963

I say to you today, my friends, so even though we face the difficulties of today and tomorrow, I still have a dream. It is a dream deeply rooted in the American dream. I have a dream that one day this nation will rise up and live out the true meaning of its creed, "We hold these truths to be self-evident, that all men are created equal."

I have a dream that one day on the red hills of Georgia, the sons of former slaves and the sons of former slave-owners will be able to sit down together at the table of brotherhood.

I have a dream that one day, even the state of Mississippi, a state sweltering with the heat of injustice, sweltering with the heat of oppression, will be transformed into an oasis of freedom and justice.

I have a dream that my four little children will one day live in a nation where they will not be judged by the color of their skin but by the content of their character. I have a dream today!

I have a dream that one day down in Alabama, with its vicious racists, with its governor having his lips dripping with the words of "interposition" and "nullification," one day right there in Alabama little black boys and black girls will be able to join hands with little white boys and white girls as sisters and brothers. I have a dream today.

I have a dream that one day "every valley shall be exalted, and every hill and mountain shall be made low; the rough places shall be made plain, and the crooked places will be made straight; and the glory of the Lord will be revealed and all flesh shall see it together."

This is our hope. This is the faith that I go back to the South with. With this faith we will be able to hew out of the mountain of despair a stone of hope. With this faith we will be able to transform the jangling discords of our nation into a beautiful symphony of brotherhood. With this faith we will be able to work together, to pray together, to struggle together, to go to jail together, to stand up for freedom together, knowing that we will be free one day. This will be the day, this will be the day when all of God's children will be able to sing with new meaning:

My country, 'tis of thee, sweet land of liberty, of thee I sing.
Land where my fathers died, land of the pilgrim's pride.
From every mountain side, let freedom ring!

And if America is to be a great nation, this must become true.

Let freedom ring from the prodigious hilltops of New Hampshire.

Let freedom ring from the mighty mountains of New York.

Let freedom ring from the heightening Alleghenies of Pennsylvania.

Let freedom ring from the snow-capped Rockies of Colorado.

Let freedom ring from the curvaceous slopes of California.

But not only that. Let freedom ring from the Stone Mountain of Georgia.

Let freedom ring from Lookout Mountain of Tennessee.

Let freedom ring from every hill and molehill of Mississippi. From every mountainside, let freedom ring.

And when this happens, when we allow freedom ring, when we let it ring from every village and hamlet, from every state and every city, we will be able to speed up that day when all of God's children, black men and white men, Jews and Gentiles, Protestants and Catholics, will be able to join hands and sing in the words of the old Negro spiritual,

Free at last! Free at last!
Thank God Almighty, we are free at last!

Robert F. Kennedy

John F. Kennedy had been president for just over 1000 days when he was assassinated in Dallas, Texas, on November 22, 1963. Nine months later the Democrats met in Atlantic City, New Jersey, to nominate Lyndon Johnson as their candidate in the 1964 presidential election. At the convention, Robert F. Kennedy, the slain president's brother who served as attorney general in both the Kennedy and Johnson administrations, gave these remarks as an introduction to a film in tribute to President Kennedy. In June 1968, while campaigning for the presidency, Robert Kennedy was also assassinated.

From His Address to the Democratic National Convention August 27, 1964

No matter what talent an individual possesses, what energy he might have, no matter how much integrity and how much honesty he might have, if he is by himself, and particularly a political figure, he can accomplish very little. But if he is sustained, as President Kennedy was, by the Democratic Party all over the United States, dedicated to the same things that he was attempting to accomplish, he can accomplish a great deal.

No one knew that more than President John F. Kennedy. He used to take great pride in telling of the trip that Thomas Jefferson and James Madison made up the Hudson River in 1800 on a botanical expedition searching for butterflies; that they ended up down in New York City and that they formed the Democratic Party.

He took great pride in the fact that the Democratic Party was the oldest political party in the world, and he knew that this linkage of Madison and Jefferson with the leaders in New York combined the North and South, and combined the industrial areas of the country with the rural farms and that this combination was always dedicated to progress and all of our Presidents have been dedicated to progress.

He thought of Thomas Jefferson in the Louisiana Purchase, and also when Jefferson realized that the United States could not remain on the Eastern Seaboard and sent Lewis and Clark to the West Coast; of Andrew Jackson; of Woodrow Wilson; of Franklin Roosevelt who saved our citizens who were in great despair because of the financial crisis; of Harry Truman who not only spoke but acted for freedom.

So, when he became President he not only had his own principles and his own ideals but he had the strength of the Democratic Party. As President he wanted to do something for the mentally ill and the mentally retarded; for those who were not covered by Social Security; for those who were not receiving an adequate minimum wage; for those who did not have adequate housing; for our elderly people who had difficulty paying their medical bills; for our fellow citizens who are not white and who had difficulty living in this society. To all this he dedicated himself.

Barbara C. Jordan

A national debate champion, Barbara Jordan's oratorical eloquence became evident in a televised hearing in 1974 when, as a member of the U. S. House of Representatives Judiciary Committee, she spoke in favor of Richard Nixon's impeachment. She was asked to give the keynote address to the Democratic National Convention in 1976, becoming the first African American of either major party to do so. Using a reflective tone and focusing on Democratic Party values as well as its mistakes, she sought to begin the healing process necessary after the traumas of Vietnam and Watergate. The speech, with her richly resonant voice, precise diction, and commanding delivery, literally electrified the delegates. It was a highlight of the convention. She retired from politics in 1979 after three terms in the House, and died in 1996.

From Her Keynote Speech, "Who Then Will Speak for the Common Good?" to the Democratic National Convention July 12, 1976

Throughout history, when people have looked for new ways to solve their problems, and to uphold the principles of this nation, many times they have turned to political parties. They have often turned to the Democratic Party.

What is it, what is it about the Democratic Party that makes it the instrument that people use when they search for ways to shape their future? Well I believe the answer to that question lies in our concept of governing. Our concept of governing is derived from our view of people. It is a concept deeply rooted in a set of beliefs firmly etched in the national conscience, of all of us. Now what are these beliefs?

First, we believe in equality for all and privileges for none. This is a belief that each American regardless of background has equal standing in the public forum, all of us. Because we believe this idea so firmly, we are inclusive rather than an exclusive party. Let everybody come.

I think it no accident that most of those emigrating to America in the 19th century identified with the Democratic Party. We are a heterogeneous party made up of Americans of diverse backgrounds.

We believe that the people are the source of all governmental power; that the authority of the people is to be extended, not restricted. This can be accomplished only by providing each citizen with every opportunity to participate in the management of the government. They must have that.

We believe that the government which represents the authority of all the people, not just one interest group, but all the people, has an obligation to actively underscore, actively seek to remove those obstacles which would block individual achievement...obstacles emanating from race, sex, economic condition. The government must seek to remove them.

We are a party of innovation. We do not reject our traditions, but we are willing to adapt to changing circumstances, when change we must. We are willing to suffer the discomfort of change in order to achieve a better future.

We have a positive vision of the future founded on the belief that the gap between the promise and reality of America can one day be finally closed. We believe that.

This, my friends, is the bedrock of our concept of governing. This is a part of the reason why Americans have turned to the Democratic Party. These are the foundations upon which a national community can be built.

James E. Carter, Jr.

In the Bicentennial year of 1976, Americans had lost their faith in government and trust of politicians. This distrust was due in large part to events in the 1960's and 1970's, including the assassinations of President John Kennedy, Dr. Martin Luther King, and Senator Robert F. Kennedy; the unpopular and divisive Vietnam War; the Watergate scandal; and the resignations of President Richard Nixon and Vice President Spiro Agnew. Americans were ready for a change and no one knew this better than Jimmy Carter, who was running for president. Carter, who had been a Naval officer, peanut farmer, businessman, and governor of Georgia, ran as a Washington outsider who promised to be a compassionate and truthful president. He won the Democratic nomination on the first ballot and chose Walter Mondale to be his running mate.

From His Nomination Acceptance Speech to the Democratic National Convention July 16, 1976

Ours is the party of the man who was nominated by those distant conventions and who inspired and restored this nation in its darkest hours – Franklin D. Roosevelt.

Ours is the party of a fighting Democrat who showed us that a common man could be an uncommon leader – Harry S. Truman.

Ours is the party of a brave young President who called the young at heart, regardless of age, to seek a "New Frontier" of national greatness – John F. Kennedy.

And ours is also the party of a great-hearted Texan who took office in a tragic hour and who went on to do more than any other President in this century to advance the cause of human rights – Lyndon Johnson.

Our party was built out of the sweatshops of the old Lower East Side, the dark mills of New Hampshire, the blazing hearths of Illinois, the coal mines of Pennsylvania, the hard-scrabble farms of the southern coastal plains, and the unlimited frontiers of America.

Ours is the party that welcomed generations of immigrants – the Jews, the Irish, the Italians, the Poles, and all the others, enlisted them in its ranks and fought the political battles that helped bring them into the American mainstream. And they have shaped the character of our party.

That is our heritage. Our party has not been perfect. We have made mistakes, and we have paid for them. But ours is a tradition of leadership and compassion and progress. Our leaders have fought for every piece of progressive legislations, from RFD to REA to Social Security and civil rights. In times of need, the Democrats were there....

During this election year we candidates will ask you for your votes, and from us will be demanded our vision.

My vision of this nation and its future has been deepened and matured during the nineteen months that I have campaigned among you for President. I have never had more faith in America than I do today. We have an America that, in Bob Dylan's phrase, is busy being born, not busy dying.

We can have an America that has reconciled its economic needs with its desire for an environment that we can pass on with pride to the next generation.

We can have an America that provides excellence in education to my child and your child and every child.

We can have an America that encourages and takes pride in our ethnic diversity, our religious diversity, our cultural diversity – knowing that out of this pluralistic heritage has come the strength and the vitality and the creativity that has made us great and will keep us great.

We can have an American government that does not oppress or spy on its own people but respects our dignity and our privacy and our right to be let alone.

We can have an America where freedom, on the one hand, and equality, on the other hand, are mutually supportive and not in conflict, and where the dreams of our nation's first leaders are fully realized in our own day and age.

And we can have an America which harnesses the idealism of the student, the compassion of a nurse or the social worker, the determination of a farmer, the wisdom of a teacher, the practicality of the business leader, the experience of the senior citizen, and the hope of a laborer to build a better life for us all. And we can have it, and we're going to have it!

As I've said many times before, we can have an American President who does not govern with negativism and fear of the future, but with vigor and vision and aggressive leadership – a President who's not isolated from the people, but who feels your pain and shares your dreams and takes his strength and his wisdom and his courage from you.

I see an America on the move again, united, a diverse and vital and tolerant nation, entering our third century with pride and confidence, an America that lives up to the majesty of our Constitution and the simple decency of our people.

This is the America we want. This is the America that we will have.

EDWARD M. KENNEDY

At the end of the 1970's, with high inflation, rising unemployment, escalating oil prices, and President Jimmy Carter's low poll numbers, many Democrats urged Senator Edward "Ted" Kennedy to enter the presidential race. On Labor Day, 1979, he did. Two months later, when the Shah of Iran was allowed into the United States to receive medical treatment, Iranian Muslim extremists seized control of the U. S. embassy in Tehran and held all of the American employees hostage. There was an outpouring of patriotism in the United States and President Carter's poll ratings went up. The support of the President by the people in a time of national crisis led Carter to win enough delegate votes in the primaries to ensure his nomination. Sen. Kennedy remained in the race until the convention, at which time he withdrew his candidacy. He died in 2009 at the age of 77, having served for 47 years in the U. S. Senate.

ADDRESS TO THE DEMOCRATIC NATIONAL CONVENTION AUGUST 12, 1980

As Democrats we recognize that each generation of Americans has a rendezvous with a different reality. The answers of one generation become the questions of the next generation. But there is a guiding star in the American firmament. It is as old as the revolutionary belief that all people are created equal, and as clear as the contemporary condition of Liberty City and the South Bronx.

Again and again Democratic leaders have followed that star and they have given new meaning to the old values of liberty and justice for all.

We are the party. We are the party of the New Freedom, the New Deal and the New Frontier. We have always been the party of hope. So this year let us offer new hope, new hope to an America uncertain about the present, but unsurpassed in its potential for the future.

To all those who are idle in the cities and industries of America, let us provide new hope for the dignity of useful work. Democrats have always believed that a basic civil right of all Americans is their right to earn their own way. The party of the people must always be the party of full employment. To all those who doubt the future of our economy, let us provide new hope for the reindustrialization of America. And let our vision reach beyond the next election or the next year to a new generation of prosperity. If we could rebuild Germany and Japan after World War II, then surely we can reindustrialize our own nation and revive our inner cities in the 1980's.

To all those who work hard for a living wage let us provide new hope that the price of their employment shall not be an unsafe workplace and a death at an earlier age.

To all those who inhabit our land from California to the New York Island, from the Redwood Forest to the Gulfstream waters, let us provide new hope that prosperity shall not be purchased by poisoning the air, the rivers and the natural resources that are the greatest gift of this continent.

We must insist that our children and our grandchildren shall inherit a land which they can truly call America the beautiful.

To all those who see the worth of their work and their savings taken by inflation, let us offer new hope for a stable economy. We must meet the pressures of the present by invoking the full power of government to master increasing prices.

In candor, we must say that the Federal budget can be balanced only by policies that bring us to a balanced prosperity of full employment and price restraint.

And to all those overburdened by an unfair tax structure, let us provide new hope for real tax reform. Instead of shutting down classrooms, let us shut off tax shelters.

Instead of cutting out school lunches, let us cut off tax subsidies for expensive business lunches that are nothing more than food stamps for the rich.

The tax cut of our Republican opponents takes the name of tax reform in vain. It is a wonderfully Republican idea that would redistribute income in the wrong direction. It is good news for any of you with incomes over $200,000 a year. For the few of you, it offers a pot of gold worth $14,000. But the Republican tax cut is bad news for the middle income families.

For the many of you, they plan a pittance of $200 a year, and that is not what the Democratic Party means when we say tax reform.

The vast majority of Americans cannot afford this panacea from a Republican nominee who has denounced the progressive income tax as the invention of Karl Marx. I am afraid he has confused Karl Marx with Theodore Roosevelt – that obscure Republican president who sought and fought for a tax system based on ability to pay. Theodore Roosevelt was not Karl Marx, and the Republican tax scheme is not tax reform.

Finally, we cannot have a fair prosperity in isolation from a fair society. So I will continue to stand for a national health insurance.

We must not surrender to the relentless medical inflation that can bankrupt almost anyone and that may soon break the budgets of government at every level. Let us insist on real control over what doctors and hospitals can charge, and let us resolve that the state of a family's health shall never depend on the size of a family's wealth.

The President, the Vice President, the members of Congress have a medical plan that meets their needs in full, and whenever senators and representatives catch a little cold, the Capitol physician will see them immediately, treat them promptly, fill a prescription on the spot. We do not get a bill even if we ask for it, and when do you think was the last time a member of Congress asked for a bill from the Federal Government?

I say again, as I have before, if health insurance is good enough for the President, the Vice President and the Congress of the United States, then it is good enough for you and every family in America.

There were some who said we should be silent about our differences on issues during this convention, but the heritage of the Democratic Party has been a history of democracy. We fight hard because we care deeply about our principles and purposes. We did not flee this struggle. We welcome the contrast with the empty and expedient spectacle last month in Detroit where no nomination was contested, no question was debated, and no one dared to raise any doubt or dissent.

Democrats can be proud that we chose a different course and a different platform. We can be proud that our party stands for investment in safe energy instead of a nuclear future that may threaten the future itself.

We must not permit the neighborhoods of America to be permanently shadowed by the fear of another Three Mile Island.

We can be proud that our party stands for a fair housing law to unlock the doors of discrimination once and for all. The American house will be divided against itself so long as there is prejudice against any American buying or renting a home.

And we can be proud that our party stands plainly and publicly and persistently for the ratification of the Equal Rights Amendment.

Women hold their rightful place at our convention, and women must have their rightful place in the Constitution of the United States. On this issue we will not yield, we will not equivocate, we will not rationalize, explain or excuse. We will stand for E.R.A. and for the recognition at long last that our nation was made up of founding mothers as well as founding fathers.

A fair prosperity and a just society are within our vision and our grasp, and we do not have every answer. There are questions not yet asked, waiting for us in the recesses of the future, but of this much we can be certain because it is the lesson of all our history: Together a president and the people can make a difference. I have found that faith still alive wherever I have traveled across this land. So let us reject the counsel of retreat and the call to reaction. Let us go forward in the knowledge that history only helps those who help themselves.

There will be setbacks and sacrifices in the years ahead; but I am convinced that we as a people are ready to give something back to our country in return for all it has given to us.

Let this be our commitment: Whatever sacrifices must be made will be shared and shared fairly. And let this be our confidence: At the end of our journey and always before us shines that ideal of liberty and justice for all....

And someday, long after this convention, long after the signs come down, and the crowds stop cheering, and the bands stop playing, may it be said of our campaign that we kept the faith. May it be said of our party in 1980 that we found our faith again.

And may it be said of us, both in dark passages and in bright days, in the words of Tennyson that my brothers quoted and loved, and that have special meaning for me now:

I am a part of all that I have met
Tho much is taken, much abides
That which we are, we are –
One equal temper of heroic hearts strong in will
To strive, to seek, to find, and not to yield.

For me, a few hours ago, this campaign came to an end. For all those whose cares have been our concern, the work goes on, the cause endures, the hope still lives, and the dream shall never die.

Walter F. Mondale

At the age of 20, Walter "Fritz" Mondale helped to manage Hubert H. Humphrey's successful 1948 election for the U. S. Senate seat from Minnesota. Ironically, when Humphrey was elected to be the Vice President in 1964, Mondale was appointed to fill Humphrey's seat in the Senate. Jimmy Carter chose Mondale to be his running mate in the 1976 presidential election, which they won. They served only one term, losing in 1980 to Ronald Reagan and George H. W. Bush. In 1984 Mondale defeated a wide range of Democratic hopefuls including Gary Hart and Jesse Jackson, Jr. to become the party's presidential candidate. In an historic move, he selected Rep. Geraldine Ferraro of New York to be his running mate, the first woman to run on the presidential ticket of a major party.

From His Nomination Acceptance Speech to the Democratic National Convention July 19, 1984

By the start of the next decade, I want to ask our children their dreams, and hear not one word about nuclear nightmares.

By the start of the next decade, I want to walk into any classroom in America and hear some of the brightest students say, "I want to be a teacher."

By the start of the next decade, I want to walk into any public health clinic in America and hear the doctor say, "We haven't seen a hungry child this year."

By the start of the next decade, I want to walk into any store in America and pick up the best product, of the best quality, at the best price; and turn it over; and read, "Made in the U.S.A."

By the start of the next decade, I want to meet with the most successful business leaders anywhere in America, and see as many minorities and women in that room as I see here in this room tonight.

By the start of the next decade, I want to point to the Supreme Court and say, "Justice is in good hands."

Before the start of the next decade, I want to go to my second Inaugural, and raise my right hand, and swear to "preserve, protect, and defend" a Constitution that includes the Equal Rights Amendment.

My friends, America is a future each generation must enlarge; a door each generation must open; a promise each generation must keep.

For the rest of my life, I want to talk to young people about their future.

And whatever their race, whatever their religion, whatever their sex, I want to hear some of them say what I say – with joy and reverence – tonight: "I want to be president of the United States."

Ann W. Richards

Ann Richards graduated from Baylor University and earned her teaching credentials at the University of Texas before teaching at the junior high school level. She volunteered to work on several Texas political campaigns, then served as a Travis County commissioner and Texas state treasurer. It was during her tenure as treasurer that she was asked in 1988 to give the Keynote Address at the Democratic National Convention. The widely-acclaimed speech is often remembered for her reference to George H. W. Bush: "Poor George. He can't help it – he was born with a silver foot in his mouth." In 1990 she was elected governor of the state of Texas and served for one term. She continued to speak out on democratic issues until her death in 2006.

From Her Keynote Address to the Democratic National Convention July 18, 1988

Now, we Democrats believe that America is still the country of fair play, that we can come out of a small town or a poor neighborhood and have the same chance as anyone else and it doesn't matter whether we are black or Hispanic or disabled or a woman.

We believe that America is a country where small business owners must succeed because they are the bedrock, backbone of our economy.

We believe that our kids deserve good day care and public schools. We believe our kids deserve public schools where students can learn, and teachers can teach.

We want to believe that our parents will have a good retirement – and that we will, too.

We Democrats believe that Social Security is a pact that cannot be broken. We want to believe that we can live out our lives without the terrible fear that an illness is going to bankrupt us and our children.

We Democrats believe that America can overcome any problem, including the dreaded disease called AIDS.

We believe that America is still a country where there is more to life than just a constant struggle for money. And we believe that America must have leaders who show us that our struggles amount to something and contribute to something larger, leaders who want us to be all that we can be.

MICHAEL S. DUKAKIS

In the 1988 presidential election, Democrats focused on Vice President George Bush's involvement in the Iran-Contra affair, the apparent unethical behavior of several members of the Reagan administration, and the economic problems resulting from huge budget deficits and the 1987 stock market collapse. Gov. Michael Dukakis of Massachusetts and Rev. Jesse Jackson led the field of candidates throughout the primaries, with Dukakis winning the nomination. Rather than campaign on the issues, the Republicans attacked Dukakis' competence and liberal values. Losing the election, Dukakis retired from politics after completing the remainder of his term as governor, going on to teach political science at several universities and serve on the Amtrak Reform Council.

FROM HIS NOMINATION ACCEPTANCE SPEECH TO THE DEMOCRATIC NATIONAL CONVENTION JULY 21, 1988

My friends, we are going to forge a new era of greatness for America.

We're going to take America's genius out of cold storage and challenge our youngsters; we're going to make our schools and universities and laboratories the finest in the world and we're going to make teaching a valued and honored profession once again.

We're going to fight fires of innovation and enterprise from coast to coast; and we're going to give those on welfare the chance to lift themselves out of poverty; to get the child care and the training they need; the chance to step out into the bright sunshine of opportunity and of hope and of dignity.

We're going to invest in our urban neighborhoods; and we're going to work to revitalize small town and rural America. We're going to give our farm families a price they can live on, and farm communities a future they can count on.

And we're going to build the kind of America that Senator Lloyd Bentsen of Texas has been fighting for 40 years; the kind of America where hard work is rewarded; where American goods and American workmanship are the best in the world and where our workers have at least 60 days notice when their plants or factories shut down.

Now, I know I have a reputation for being a frugal man. In nine years, I've balanced nine more budgets than this Administration has and I've just balanced a tenth. And I've worked with the citizens of my state, worked hard to create hundreds of new jobs, and I mean good jobs, jobs you can raise a family on, jobs you can build a future on, jobs you can count on.

I'm proud of our progress, but I'm even prouder of the way we've made that progress – by working together; by excluding no one and including everyone: business and labor; educators and community leaders and just plain citizens – sharing responsibility; exchanging ideas; building confidence about the future.

And what we have done reflects a simple but very profound idea – an idea as powerful as any in human history.

It is the idea of community.

It is the idea that we are in this together; that regardless of who we are or where we come from or how much money we have – each of us counts. And that by working together to create opportunity and a good life for all – all of us are enriched – not just in economic terms, but as citizens and as human beings.

WILLIAM J. CLINTON

With an approval rating of 91% and a victory in the Persian Gulf War in early 1991, George H. W. Bush looked like a shoo-in for re-election in 1992. This strength in the polls led several strong Democratic contenders, including Mario Cuomo and Al Gore, not to enter the race. However, by August, Bush's approval ratings had dropped precipitously to 29% due an economic downturn. Gov. William J. Clinton of Arkansas was one of the relative unknowns seeking the Democratic nomination in 1992. A Rhodes Scholar and Yale Law School graduate, he had been elected governor in 1978 at the age of 32. Claiming to be a more centrist "new Democrat," Clinton called for a new covenant that paired opportunity with responsibility. He won the nomination after a hard-fought primary season with Paul Tsongas as his main opponent. Selecting Al Gore of Tennessee as his running mate, Clinton went on to become the first "baby-boomer" President of the United States.

FROM HIS NOMINATION ACCEPTANCE SPEECH TO THE DEMOCRATIC NATIONAL CONVENTION JULY 16, 1992

Somewhere at this very moment, another child is born in America. Let it be our cause to give that child a happy home, a healthy family, a hopeful future. Let it be our cause to see that child reach the fullest of her God-given abilities.

Let it be our cause that she grow up strong and secure, braced by her challenges, but never, never struggling alone; with family and friends and a faith that in American, no one is left out; no one is left behind.

Let it be our cause that when she is able, she gives something back to her children, her community, and her country. And let it be our cause to give her a country that's coming together, and moving ahead – a country of boundless hopes and endless dreams.

A country that once again lifts up its people, and inspires the world.

Let that be our cause and our commitment and our New Covenant.

HAROLD E. FORD, JR.

1996 was a big year for Harold Ford, Jr. – he graduated from the University of Michigan Law School and ran for the 9th District seat in the U. S. House of Representatives. Even though the seat he was seeking had been held by his father for 22 years, Rep. Ford still had trouble getting speaking engagements in his district. About the only invitations he received were for kindergarten graduations. He accepted all these invitations – 30 of them – because "for those children and their families, we must continue working for a better life and a better world." Harold Ford won that election and three more. At the 2000 Democratic National Convention, at the age of 30, he became the youngest person to be a keynote speaker. In that speech he spoke of those kindergarten graduations as well as his vision of the future.

FROM HIS KEYNOTE ADDRESS TO THE DEMOCRATIC NATIONAL CONVENTION AUGUST 15, 2000

We have a very different vision of the future....

Imagine a debt-free economy so strong that everyone shares in the American Dream.

Imagine a healthcare system where every American receives the medicine they need, and where no senior is forced to choose between buying food and filling a prescription.

Imagine a society that treats seniors with the respect and dignity they deserve, and where Social Security and Medicare are strengthened, not only for our parents and grandparents, but for our children and grandchildren.

Imagine a nation of clean coastlines, safe drinking water, pristine parks, and air our kids can breathe as they play in those parks.

We all recognize that no issue is more critical to our nation's continued success than how we educate our kids.

If we can find the will and resources to build prison after prison, then we can build new schools, reduce class sizes, connect every classroom up to the Internet. Surely we can pay teachers what they are worth – surely we must hold schools accountable for results. Imagine giving all our kids the world-class education they deserve.

Well, it is time to stop imagining. So tonight I call on all my reform-minded Republican and Independent friends to join us in our crusade. To join us in making this bold imagination a reality.

JOHN E. BALDACCI

A graduate of the University of Maine, John Baldacci began his political career at the age of 23 when he was elected to the Bangor, Maine city council. Four years later, he won a seat in the state Senate and in 1994 ran for the U. S. Congress, serving four terms. In 2002, he was elected governor of Maine, the office he currently holds.

WHY I AM A DEMOCRAT
RESPONSE TO THE AUTHOR'S REQUEST
AUGUST 6, 2003

Regardless of party affiliation, I believe each citizen should take an active interest in public policy issues, our governmental institutions and the electoral process. Whether a Democrat, Republican, member of another party, or unenrolled voter, it's important to be informed, concerned and involved. My father was a strong supporter of President Kennedy's campaign in 1960. Since that time, I have appreciated the Democratic Party's focus on education, health care, environmental protection and issues of special concern to older Americans. Being a Democrat means striving to strengthen our families, communities and nation. It means seeking to enhance our economy and security – by working collaboratively with others to arrive at common ground and workable solutions.

EDWARD ASNER

Edward Asner has appeared off-Broadway and in films, but is best known for his work in television. He won three Emmys for his role as Lou Grant on the Mary Tyler Moore Show, *and another Emmy for his part in the* Roots *miniseries. Active politically, he was elected twice as the president of the Screen Actors Guild.*

WHY I AM A DEMOCRAT
RESPONSE TO THE AUTHOR'S REQUEST
AUGUST 25, 2003

The wry comment I usually make is that Conservatives are necessary to conserve the societal advances and progress that Liberals achieve. And to me now especially, the only major hope for Liberals is the Democratic Party. At the same time, I'm driven to madness at the ineffectualness and lack of boldness on the part of so many Democrats who are busily attempting to be Republican 'lite.'

I have always been a Democrat and until something more liberal and potentially successful comes along, I'll die a Democrat. I am one primarily because it is a party that concerns itself with the people – helping far more of the masses than the other guys. The Democratic Party has been responsible for pushing through almost all of the beneficial social legislation that has come down in the last 80 years. It has had a farther reaching foreign policy than the Republican Party and it concerns itself with more than the rich and the reduction of taxes. Its main drawback has been a lack of aversion to war but an improved Democratic Party will achieve that as well. It is a party that works to employ, educate, nurture, house and safeguard as many of the people as they can while still providing the freedoms guaranteed at our nation's founding. If only campaign financing were controlled in this country, the Democrats would always be a majority party.

PROGRESS

WE ARE DETERMINED TO MAKE EVERY AMERICAN CITIZEN THE SUBJECT OF HIS COUNTRY'S INTEREST AND CONCERN; AND WE WILL NEVER REGARD ANY FAITHFUL LAW-ABIDING GROUP WITHIN OUR BORDERS AS SUPERFLUOUS. THE TEST OF OUR PROGRESS IS NOT WHETHER WE ADD MORE TO THE ABUNDANCE OF THOSE WHO HAVE MUCH; IT IS WHETHER WE PROVIDE ENOUGH FOR THOSE WHO HAVE TOO LITTLE.

Franklin D. Roosevelt
Second Inaugural Address
January 20, 1937

WOODROW WILSON

Woodrow Wilson was president of Princeton University when he was elected governor of New Jersey in 1910. Two years later, he was nominated to be the Democratic candidate for President of the United States. He ran against the Republican incumbent William Howard Taft, the Progressive Party candidate Theodore Roosevelt, and the Socialist Party candidate, Eugene Debs. His New Freedom platform focused on breaking the trusts – businesses that through mergers with or acquisitions of other businesses effectively restricted competition – so that a free flow of enterprise would flourish. Roosevelt and Taft split the Republican vote, and Wilson won the election with 41% of the popular vote.

In 1916 Wilson ran for re-election against Supreme Court Justice Charles Evans Hughes on a platform of continued progressivism and peace. In his first term, which focused primarily on domestic issues, Wilson had effectively broken the trusts through three major pieces of legislation: The Underwood Tariff Reform Act, the Federal Reserve Act, and the Clayton Antitrust Act. Wilson was re-elected by a narrow margin. Despite his attempts at neutrality, the United States entered World War I in April 1917. His second term focused on international issues – primarily the war and the League of Nations.

FROM HIS FIRST INAUGURAL ADDRESS
MARCH 4, 1913

There has been a change of government. It began two years ago, when the House of Representatives became Democratic by a decisive majority. It has now been completed. The Senate about to assemble will also be Democratic. The offices of President and Vice-President have been put into the hands of Democrats. What does the change mean? That is the question that is uppermost in our minds today. That is the question I am going to try to answer, in order, if I may, to interpret the occasion....

It means much more than the mere success of a party. The success of a party means little except when the Nation is using that party for a large and definite purpose. No one can mistake the purpose for which the Nation now seeks to use the Democratic Party. It seeks to use it to interpret a change in its own plans and point of view. Some old things with which we had grown familiar, and which had begun to creep into the very habit of our thought and of our lives, have altered their aspect as we have latterly looked critically upon them, with fresh, awakened eyes; have dropped their disguises and shown themselves alien and sinister. Some new things, as we look frankly upon them, willing to comprehend their real character, have come to assume the aspect of things long believed in and familiar, stuff of our own convictions. We have been refreshed by a new insight into our life.

FROM HIS SECOND INAUGURAL ADDRESS
MARCH 4, 1917

The four years which have elapsed since last I stood in this place have been crowded with counsel and action of the most vital interest and consequence. Perhaps no equal period in our history has been so fruitful of important reforms in our economic and industrial life or so full of significant changes in the spirit and purpose of our political action. We have sought very thoughtfully to set our house in order, correct the grosser errors and abuses of our industrial life, liberate and quicken the processes of our national genius and energy, and lift our politics to a broader view of the people's essential interests. It is a record of singular variety and singular distinction. But I shall not attempt to review it. It speaks for itself and will be of increasing influence as the years go by.

MAJOR ACCOMPLISHMENTS

- ***19th Constitutional Amendment*** gave women the right to vote.
- ***Clayton Anti-Trust Act*** expanded the Sherman Anti-Trust Act's list of objectionable business practices and exempted labor and agricultural organizations from anti-trust prosecution.
- ***Federal Farm Loan Act*** provided low-interest loans to farmers.
- ***Federal Reserve Banking System*** created a system of 12 regional reserve banks.
- ***Federal Trade Commission Act*** focused on unfair trade practices in interstate commerce.
- ***Keating Owen Child Labor Act*** prohibited interstate shipping of products produced by children.

FRANKLIN D. ROOSEVELT

Franklin Roosevelt was born into a prominent, wealthy family and was taught that he had a responsibility to help those who were less fortunate. His opponent in the 1932 presidential election was the incumbent Herbert Hoover, who believed in the trickle down economic theory that government aid given to those at the top of the economic pyramid would ultimately create more jobs for those at the bottom. This was in marked contrast to Roosevelt's belief that government assistance should be given to the "little fellow" and would spur the economy from the bottom up rather than the top down. He went on to defeat Hoover and put his beliefs into action through his New Deal, which he outlined in this speech before the Democratic National Convention.

FROM HIS NOMINATION ACCEPTANCE SPEECH TO THE DEMOCRATIC NATIONAL CONVENTION JULY 2, 1932

There are two ways of viewing the Government's duty in matters affecting economic and social life. The first sees to it that a favored few are helped and hopes that some of their prosperity will leak through, sift through, to labor, to the farmer, to the small businessman. That theory belongs to the party of Toryism, and I had hoped that most of the Tories left this country in 1776. But it is not and never will be the theory of the Democratic Party.... Ours must be a party of liberal thought, of planned action, of enlightened international outlook, and of the greatest good to the greatest number of our citizens....

Never before in modern history have the essential differences between the two major American parties stood out in such striking contrast as they do today. Republican leaders not only have failed in material things, they have failed in national vision, because in disaster they have held out no hope, they have pointed out no path for the people below to climb back to places of security and of safety in our American life.

Throughout the nation, men and women, forgotten in the political philosophy of the government of the last years, look to us here for guidance and for more equitable opportunity to share in the distribution of national wealth.

On the farms, in the large metropolitan areas, in the smaller cities and in the villages, millions of our citizens cherish the hope that their old standards of living and of thought have not gone forever. Those millions cannot and shall not hope in vain.

I pledge you, I pledge myself, to a New Deal for the American people. Let us all here assembled constitute ourselves prophets of a new order of competence and of courage. This is more than a political campaign; it is a call to arms. Give me your help, not to win votes alone, but to win in this crusade to restore America to its own people.

MAJOR ACCOMPLISHMENTS

- ***Civilian Conservation Corps*** employed three million young men during the Depression.
- ***Fair Labor Standards Act*** established minimum wages, maximum working hours, and limits to child labor.
- ***Farm Security Administration*** provided low interest loans to tenant farmers.
- ***Federal Securities Act*** required sellers of securities to provide truthful information about value of investments.
- ***GI Bill of Rights*** provided Federal government aid for the readjustment in civilian life of returning World War II veterans.
- ***Glass-Steagall Banking Act*** created the Federal Deposit Insurance Corporation to prevent bank failures.

- ***Lend-Lease Act*** allowed the U.S., prior to its entry into World War II, to send arms to its allies who would either return or pay for them once the war was over.
- ***National Labor Relations Act*** allowed labor to organize and bargain collectively.
- ***Public Works Administration*** attempted to revive industry and reduce unemployment through public construction projects.
- ***Securities Exchange Commission*** protected the public against securities fraud.
- ***Social Security Act***, which was financed by a payroll tax, provided unemployment insurance, old age pensions, and support for the blind, handicapped, and dependent children.
- ***Tennessee Valley Authority*** developed a series of hydroelectric generating dams to provide employment in a severely depressed area and reform power company monopolies.
- ***Works Project Administration*** created public jobs for the unemployed during the Depression.

HARRY S. TRUMAN

Harry Truman believed the federal government was responsible for providing for the security, health, education, and civil rights of its citizens, concerns that he expressed in his State of the Union Addresses in 1947 and 1948. In his State of the Union Address in 1949, he reiterated these domestic goals and labeled them the "Fair Deal." With Republicans and southern Democrats opposing most of Truman's program, only an increase in the minimum wage, the 1949 Housing Act, and the 1950 Social Security Act were passed.

FROM HIS STATE OF THE UNION MESSAGE
JANUARY 5, 1949

The Government has still other opportunities – to help raise the standard of living of our citizens. These opportunities lie in the fields of social security, health, education, housing, and civil rights.

The present coverage of the social security laws is altogether inadequate; the benefit payments are too low. One-third of our workers are not covered. Those who receive old-age and survivors insurance benefits receive an average payment of only $25 a month. Many others who cannot work because they are physically disabled are left to the mercy of charity. We should expand our social security program, both as to the size of the benefits and the extent of coverage, against the economic hazards due to unemployment, old age, sickness, and disability.

We must spare no effort to raise the general level of health in this country. In a nation as rich as ours, it is a shocking fact that tens of millions lack adequate medical care. We are short of doctors, hospitals, and nurses. We must remedy these shortages. Moreover, we need – and we must have without further delay – a system of prepaid medical insurance which will enable every American to afford good medical care.

It is equally shocking that millions of our children are not receiving a good education. Millions of them are in overcrowded, obsolete buildings. We are short of teachers, because teachers' salaries are too low to attract new teachers, or to hold the ones we have. All these school problems will become much more acute as a result of the tremendous increase in the enrollment in our elementary schools in the next few years. I cannot repeat too strongly my desire for prompt Federal financial aid to the States to help them operate and maintain their school systems....

The driving force behind our progress is our faith in our democratic institutions. That faith is embodied in the promise of equal rights and equal opportunities which the founders of our Republic proclaimed to their countrymen and to the whole world.

The fulfillment of this promise is among the highest purposes of government. The civil rights proposals I made to the 80th Congress, I now repeat to the 81st Congress. They should be enacted in order that the Federal Government may assume the leadership and discharge the obligations clearly placed upon it by the Constitution.

We stand at the opening of an era which can mean either great achievement or terrible catastrophe for ourselves and for all mankind.

The strength of our Nation must continue to be used in the interest of all our people rather than a privileged few. It must continue to be used unselfishly in the struggle for world peace and the betterment of mankind the world over.

This is the task before us. It is not an easy one. It has many complications, and there will be strong opposition from selfish interests. I hope for cooperation from farmers, from labor, and from business. Every segment of our population and every individual has a right to expect from our Government a fair deal.

MAJOR ACCOMPLISHMENTS

- ***Atomic Energy Act*** created the Atomic Energy Commission to regulate and oversee the development of nuclear technology.
- ***Communicable Disease Center*** (now Centers for Disease Control and Prevention) monitored and controlled infectious diseases.
- ***Employment Act*** established the Council of Economic Advisors and promoted maximum employment, production, and purchasing power.
- ***Fair Housing Act*** provided Federal aid for slum clearance, community development, and redevelopment programs.
- ***Labor Standards Act Amendments*** raised the minimum wage to $.75 per hour and extended coverage.
- ***The Marshall Plan*** provided U. S. financial assistance following World War II to 16 European countries that agreed to formulate a joint plan for their economic recovery.
- ***North Atlantic Treaty Organization*** was an alliance between 11 European countries and the United States to contain the Soviet Union and integrate Germany back into post-war Europe.
- ***Organization of American States*** promoted inner-American cooperation through a charter signed by 21 western hemisphere nations.
- ***President's Commission on Civil Rights*** was established by Truman following the murder of six African American war veterans. The commission's recommendations led Truman to desegregate the Federal civil service system and the U. S. armed forces.
- ***Social Security Act Amendments*** extended benefits to an additional 10 million people.
- ***The Truman Doctrine*** established that the United States would provide political, military and economic assistance to all democratic nations under threat from external or internal authoritarian forces.

JOHN F. KENNEDY

John F. Kennedy came to the 1960 presidential race as a war hero who had been elected to the U. S. House of Representatives three times and to the U. S. Senate twice. He had won the Pulitzer Prize in history for his book Profiles in Courage. *Through his nomination acceptance speech, he wanted to establish in his campaign a sense of national purpose and commitment – challenging Americans to become the pioneers in a New Frontier of "opportunities and perils" of the 1960's.*

NOMINATION ACCEPTANCE SPEECH TO THE DEMOCRATIC NATIONAL CONVENTION JULY 15, 1960

For I stand tonight facing west on what was once the last frontier. From the lands that stretch three thousand miles behind me, the pioneers of old gave up their safety, their comfort and sometimes their lives to build a new world here in the West. They were not the captives of their own doubts, the prisoners of their own price tags. Their motto was not "every man for himself" – but "all for the common cause." They were determined to make that new world strong and free, to overcome its hazards and its hardships, to conquer the enemies that threatened from without and within.

Today some would say that those struggles are all over – that all the horizons have been explored – that all the battles have been won – that there is no longer an American frontier.

But I trust that no one in this vast assemblage will agree with those sentiments. For the problems are not all solved and the battles are not all won – and we stand today on the edge of a New Frontier – the frontier of the 1960's – a frontier of unknown opportunities and perils – a frontier of unfulfilled hopes and threats.

Woodrow Wilson's New Freedom promised our nation a new political and economic framework. Franklin Roosevelt's New Deal promised security and succor to those in need. But the New Frontier of which I speak is not a set of promises – it is a set of challenges. It sums up not what I intend to offer the American people, but what I intend to ask of them. It appeals to their pride, not to their pocketbook – it holds out the promise of more sacrifice instead of more security.

But I tell you the New Frontier is here, whether we seek it or not. Beyond that frontier are the uncharted areas of science and space, unsolved problems of peace and war, unconquered pockets of ignorance and prejudice, unanswered questions of poverty and surplus. It would be easier to shrink back from that frontier, to look to the safe mediocrity of the past, to be lulled by good intentions and high rhetoric – and those who prefer that course should not cast their votes for me, regardless of party.

But I believe the times demand new invention, innovation, imagination, decision. I am asking each of you to be pioneers on that New Frontier. My call is to the young in heart, regardless of age – to all who respond to the Scriptural call: "Be strong and of a good courage; be not afraid, neither be thou dismayed."

For courage – not complacency – is our need today – leadership – not salesmanship. And the only valid test of leadership is the ability to lead, and lead vigorously. A tired nation, said David Lloyd George, is a Tory nation – and the United States today cannot afford to be either tired or Tory.

There may be those who wish to hear more – more promises to this group or that – more harsh rhetoric about the men in the Kremlin – more assurances of a golden future, where taxes are always low and subsidies ever high. But my promises are in the platform you have adopted – our ends will not be won by rhetoric and we can have faith in the future only if we have faith in ourselves.

For the harsh facts of the matter are that we stand on this frontier at a turning-point in history. We must prove all over again whether this nation – or any nation so conceived – can long endure – whether our society – with its freedom of choice, its breadth of opportunity, its range of alternatives – can compete with the single-minded advance of the Communist system.

Can a nation organized and governed such as ours endure? That is the real question. Have we the nerve and the will? Can we carry through in an age where we will witness not only new breakthroughs in weapons of destruction – but also a race for mastery of the sky and the rain, the ocean and the tides, the far side of space and the inside of men's minds?

Are we up to the task – are we equal to the challenge? Are we willing to match the Russian sacrifice of the present for the future – or must we sacrifice our future in order to enjoy the present?

That is the question of the New Frontier. That is the choice our nation must make – a choice that lies not merely between two men or two parties, but between the public interest and private comfort – between national greatness and national decline – between the fresh air of progress and the stale, dank atmosphere of "normalcy" – between determined dedication and creeping mediocrity.

All mankind waits upon our decision. A whole world looks to see what we will do. We cannot fail their trust, we cannot fail to try.

MAJOR ACCOMPLISHMENTS

- ***Alliance for Progress*** gave economic aid to Latin America in an attempt to thwart the spread of communism into those countries.
- ***Federal Clean Air Act*** provided for the definition of air quality criteria by the Department of Health, Education, and Welfare, and grants to state and local air pollution control agencies.

- ***Limited Test Ban Treaty*** between U. S., Great Britain, and Soviet Union banned nuclear weapons testing in the atmosphere, outer space, and under water.
- ***NASA Program*** accelerated the goal to land a man on the Moon.
- ***Peace Corps*** promoted peace through American volunteers who brought their skills to developing nations.
- ***Trade Expansion Act*** authorized tariff cuts of 50% with the European Common Market.

Lyndon B. Johnson

A few days after taking office as President of the United States, Lyndon Johnson urged Americans to continue the work that slain President John F. Kennedy had begun, including a tax cut and a civil rights bill. Once these were passed into law, Johnson laid out his domestic agenda, which he referred to as the "Great Society." In 1965, the Democrats controlled the White House and both houses of Congress, and American society was ready for social reform. Johnson pushed through a mass of legislation, the cornerstones of which were education, health care, civil rights, and the war on poverty. Incredibly, by the end of 1965 most of this reform legislation was passed into law.

From His Speech, "The Great Society," at the University of Michigan May 22, 1964

I have come today from the turmoil of your Capital to the tranquility of your campus to speak about the future of your country.

The purpose of protecting the life of our Nation and preserving the liberty of our citizens is to pursue the happiness of our people. Our success in that pursuit is the test of our success as a Nation.

For a century we labored to settle and to subdue a continent. For half a century we called upon unbounded invention and untiring industry to create an order of plenty for all of our people.

The challenge of the next half century is whether we have the wisdom to use that wealth to enrich and elevate our national life, and to advance the quality of our American civilization.

Your imagination, your initiative, and your indignation will determine whether we build a society where progress is the servant of our needs, or a society where old values and new visions are buried under unbridled growth. For in your time we have the opportunity to move not only toward the rich society and the powerful society, but upward to the Great Society.

The Great Society rests on abundance and liberty for all. It demands an end to poverty and racial injustice, to which we are totally committed in our time. But that is just the beginning.

The Great Society is a place where every child can find knowledge to enrich his mind and to enlarge his talents. It is a place where leisure is a welcome chance to build and reflect, not a feared cause of boredom and restlessness. It is a place where the city of man serves not only the needs of the body and the demands of commerce but the desire for beauty and the hunger for community.

It is a place where man can renew contact with nature. It is a place which honors creation for its own sake and for what it adds to the understanding of the race. It is a place where men are more concerned with the quality of their goals than the quantity of their goods.

But most of all, the Great Society is not a safe harbor, a resting place, a final objective, a finished work. It is a challenge constantly renewed, beckoning us toward a destiny where the meaning of our lives matches the marvelous products of our labor.

For better or worse, your generation has been appointed by history to deal with those problems and to lead America toward a new age. You have the chance never before afforded to any people at any age. You can help build a society where the demands of morality, the needs of the spirit, can be realized in the life of the Nation.

So, will you join in the battle to give every citizen the full equality which God enjoins and the law requires, whatever his belief, or race, or the color of his skin? Will you join in the battle to give every citizen an escape from the crushing weight of poverty?

Will you join in the battle to make it possible for all nations to live in enduring peace – as neighbors and not as mortal enemies?

Will you join in the battle to build the Great Society, to prove that our material progress is only the foundation on which we will build a richer life of mind and spirit?

There are those timid souls who say this battle cannot be won; that we are condemned to a soulless wealth. I do not agree. We have the power to shape the civilization that we want. But we need your will, your labor, your hearts, if we are to build that kind of society.

Those who came to this land sought to build more than just a new country.

They sought a new world. So I have come here today to your campus to say that you can make their vision our reality. So let us from this moment begin our work so that in the future men will look back and say: It was then, after a long and weary way, that man turned the exploits of his genius to the full enrichment of his life.

Major Accomplishments

- ***Affirmative Action Executive Order*** required Federal contractors to take affirmative action against discrimination.
- ***Civil Rights Acts of 1964*** prohibited discrimination in public facilities.
- ***Department of Transportation and Department of Housing and Urban Development*** established.
- ***Elementary and Secondary School Act*** provided funds and guidance to K-12 schools.
- ***Equal Employment Opportunity Commission*** sought to eliminate discrimination in hiring.
- ***Equal Opportunity Act*** provided for programs such as VISTA (Volunteers in Service to America), Job Corps, Upward Bound, Head Start, Foster Grandparents, and Legal Services as part of the War on Poverty.

- ***Higher Education Act*** strengthened education resources of colleges and universities, and provided financial assistance for students in post-secondary and higher education.
- ***Highway Safety Act*** created a partnership between national, state, and local governments to improve highway safety.
- ***Immigration Act*** abolished national origins quota system, increased the number of immigrants allowed to enter U. S. annually, and limited the number of immigrants from the western hemisphere.
- ***Land and Water Conservation Act*** provided matching grants to state and local governments to acquire and develop public outdoor recreation areas and facilities.
- ***Medicare and Medicaid*** provided health care for the elderly and poor.
- ***National Foundation for the Arts and Humanities*** promoted American culture.
- ***National Historic Preservation Act*** established a program to preserve historic properties throughout the nation.
- ***National Traffic and Motor Vehicle Safety Act*** authorized the U. S. government to set and regulate standards for motor vehicles and highways in order to promote safety and decrease motor vehicle related fatalities and injuries.
- ***Public Broadcasting System*** authorized the Corporation for Public Broadcasting to assist in the development of a nationwide public broadcasting system.
- ***Truth-in-Lending Act*** protected consumers in credit transactions.
- ***Voting Rights Act*** prohibited discrimination in voting practices or procedures on the basis of race or color.
- ***Wild and Scenic Rivers Act*** preserved and protected certain rivers and their immediate environments for the benefit and enjoyment of Americans.
- ***Wilderness Act*** established a National Wilderness Preservation System of federally owned wilderness areas.

JAMES E. CARTER, JR.

The election of 1976 pitted the incumbent Gerald Ford, a long-time Washington insider, against Jimmy Carter, a relatively unknown Washington outsider. Ford, who had assumed the office when President Nixon resigned in 1974, campaigned on fighting inflation. Carter, well ahead in the polls when the campaign began, focused on reducing unemployment. By November the race had become quite close. However, the poor economy as well as Ford's association with and pardon of Nixon gave Carter the edge and a narrow victory.

FROM HIS INAUGURAL ADDRESS
JANUARY 20, 1977

Within us, the people of the United States, there is evident a serious and purposeful rekindling of confidence. And I join in the hope that when my time as your President has ended, people might say this about our Nation:

- That we had remembered the words of Micah and renewed our search for humility, mercy, and justice;
- That we had torn down the barriers that separated those of different race and region and religion, and where there had been mistrust, built unity, with a respect for diversity;
- That we had found productive work for those able to perform it;
- That we had strengthened the American family, which is the basis of our society;
- That we had ensured respect for the law, and equal treatment under the law, for the weak and the powerful, for the rich and the poor;

- And that we had enabled our people to be proud of their own Government once again.

I would hope that the nations of the world might say that we had built a lasting peace, built not on weapons of war but on international policies which reflect our own most precious values.

These are not just my goals, and they will not be my accomplishments, but the affirmation of our Nation's continuing moral strength and our belief in an undiminished, ever-expanding American dream.

MAJOR ACCOMPLISHMENTS

- ***Alaskan Wilderness Area*** was designated covering, 100 million acres.
- ***Camp David Accords*** was an agreement between Egypt and Israel mediated by President Carter, establishing a framework for peace in the Middle East.
- ***Department of Education and Department of Energy*** established.
- ***Federal Emergency Management Agency*** established to centralize Federal disaster-related emergency functions.
- ***Humphrey-Hawkins Full Employment Act*** stated that every American has the right to useful employment at a fair rate of pay, and required the Chairman of the Federal Reserve Board to testify before Congress twice each year regarding the state of the economy.
- ***S.A.L.T. II*** was an agreement between the Soviet Union and the United States limiting the number and development of strategic nuclear delivery vehicles in each country.
- ***Superfund*** established to clean up hazardous toxic waste dumps.

WILLIAM J. CLINTON

The presidential election of 1992 was a three-man race between Gov. William J. Clinton of Arkansas, incumbent President George H. W. Bush, and Texas billionaire Ross Perot. The Clinton campaign focused on welfare reform, health care, and the economy. The "war room" at Clinton headquarters was primed to give a rapid response to Republican attacks on Clinton's record and character, thereby neutralizing their effect on the electorate. The election was a clean sweep for the Democrats, who won the White House as well as majorities in both houses of Congress.

FROM HIS FIRST INAUGURAL ADDRESS
JANUARY 20, 1993

We know we have to face hard truths and take strong steps, but we have not done so. Instead we have drifted, and that drifting has eroded our resources, fractured our economy, and shaken our confidence. Though our challenges are fearsome, so are our strengths. Americans have ever been a restless, questing, hopeful people, and we must bring to our task today the vision and will of those who came before us. From our Revolution to the Civil War, to the Great Depression, to the Civil Rights movement, our people have always mustered the determination to construct from these crises the pillars of our history. Thomas Jefferson believed that to preserve the very foundations of our nation we would need dramatic change from time to time. Well, my fellow Americans, this is our time. Let us embrace it.

Our democracy must be not only the envy of the world but the engine of our own renewal. There is nothing wrong with America that cannot be cured by what is right with America. And so today we pledge an end to the era of deadlock and drift, and a new season of American renewal has begun.

To renew America, we must be bold. We must do what no generation has had to do before. We must invest more in our own people, in their jobs, and in their future, and at the same time cut our massive debt. And we must do so in a world in which we must compete for every opportunity. It will not be easy. It will require sacrifice. But it can be done, and done fairly. Not choosing sacrifice for its own sake, but for our own sake. We must provide for our nation the way a family provides for its children.

Our founders saw themselves in the light of posterity. We can do no less. Anyone who has ever watched a child's eyes wander into sleep knows what posterity is. Posterity is the world to come, the world for whom we hold our ideals, from whom we have borrowed our planet, and to whom we bear sacred responsibilities. We must do what America does best, offer more opportunity to all and demand more responsibility from all.

MAJOR ACCOMPLISHMENTS

- ***Crime Bill*** provided grants to put 100,000 police officers on the streets, expanded death penalty offences, and banned the manufacture of certain deadly assault weapons.

- ***Drunk Driving Law*** set the blood alcohol limit for drunkenness at 0.08% in order to reduce alcohol-related accidents.

- ***Family and Medical Leave Act*** offered 42 million Americans up to 12 weeks unpaid, job-guaranteed leave for the birth or adoption of a child, or personal or family illness.

- ***Goals 2000 Education Bill*** provided Federal grants to raise academic standards and improve schools.

- ***Handgun Waiting Period Bill (Brady Bill)*** instituted a five-day waiting period on handgun purchases so that background checks could be done.

- ***NAFTA*** was an agreement between the U. S., Canada, and Mexico to eliminate trade barriers while promoting fair competition.
- ***National Service Act (AmeriCorps)*** established a network of national service programs in which volunteers worked either full- or part-time for up to a year in return for an education award or end-of-service stipend.
- ***Voter Registration Act (Motor Voter)*** facilitated voter registration and placed limitations on removal of voters from registration lists.
- ***Welfare Reform Act*** changed the nation's welfare system by requiring work in exchange for time-limited financial assistance.

BARACK H. OBAMA

In the 2008 presidential election, for the first time in 56 years, an incumbent president or vice president was not a candidate. The wide-open contest initially included nine Democratic and twelve Republican presidential candidates. Senators Hillary Clinton and Barack Obama emerged as the Democratic frontrunners, with Obama clinching the nomination in June. Senator John McCain won the Republican nomination. With the major campaign issues being the wars in Iraq and Afghanistan, and the floundering economy, both Clinton and McCain claimed the importance of their political experience, while Obama focused his message on bringing change to Washington. On November 4th, Barack Obama became the first African American to be elected President of the United States.

FROM HIS INAUGURAL ADDRESS
JANUARY 20, 2009

Forty-four Americans have now taken the presidential oath. The words have been spoken during rising tides of prosperity and the still waters of peace. Yet, every so often, the oath is taken amidst gathering clouds and raging storms. At these moments, America has carried on not simply because of the skill or vision of those in high office, but because we, the people, have remained faithful to the ideals of our forebears and true to our founding documents.

So it has been; so it must be with this generation of Americans.

That we are in the midst of crisis is now well understood. Our nation is at war against a far-reaching network of violence and hatred. Our economy is badly weakened, a consequence of greed and irresponsibility on the part of some, but also our collective failure to make hard choices and prepare the nation for a new age. Homes have been lost, jobs shed, businesses shuttered. Our health care is too costly, our schools fail too many – and each day brings further evidence that the ways we use energy strengthen our adversaries and threaten our planet.

These are the indicators of crisis, subject to data and statistics. Less measurable, but no less profound, is a sapping of confidence across our land; a nagging fear that America's decline is inevitable, that the next generation must lower its sights.

Today I say to you that the challenges we face are real. They are serious and they are many. They will not be met easily or in a short span of time. But know this America: They will be met.

On this day, we gather because we have chosen hope over fear, unity of purpose over conflict and discord. On this day, we come to proclaim an end to the petty grievances and false promises, the recriminations and worn-out dogmas that for far too long have strangled our politics. We remain a young nation. But in the words of Scripture, the time has come to set aside childish things. The time has come to reaffirm our enduring spirit; to choose our better history; to carry forward that precious gift, that noble idea passed on from generation to generation: the God-given promise that all are equal, all are free, and all deserve a chance to pursue their full measure of happiness.

In reaffirming the greatness of our nation we understand that greatness is never a given. It must be earned. Our journey has never been one of short-cuts or settling for less. It has not been the path for the faint-hearted, for those that prefer leisure over work, or seek only the pleasures of riches and fame. Rather, it has been the risk-takers, the doers, the makers of things – some celebrated, but more often men and women obscure in their labor – who have carried us up the long rugged path towards prosperity and freedom.

For us, they packed up their few worldly possessions and traveled across oceans in search of a new life. For us, they toiled in sweatshops, and settled the West, endured the lash of the whip, and plowed the hard earth. For us, they fought and died in places like Concord and Gettysburg, Normandy and Khe Sahn.

Time and again these men and women struggled and sacrificed and worked till their hands were raw so that we might live a better life. They saw America as bigger than the sum of our individual ambitions, greater than all the differences of birth or wealth or faction.

This is the journey we continue today. We remain the most prosperous, powerful nation on Earth. Our workers are no less productive than when this crisis began. Our minds are no less inventive, our goods and services no less needed than they were last week, or last month, or last year. Our capacity remains undiminished. But our time of standing pat, of protecting narrow interests and putting off unpleasant decisions – that time has surely passed. Starting today, we must pick ourselves up, dust ourselves off, and begin again the work of remaking America.

For everywhere we look, there is work to be done. The state of our economy calls for action, bold and swift. And we will act, not only to create new jobs, but to lay a new foundation for growth. We will build the roads and bridges, the electric grids and digital lines that feed our commerce and bind us together. We'll restore science to its rightful place, and wield technology's wonders to raise health care's quality and lower its cost. We will harness the sun and the winds and the soil to fuel our cars and run our factories. And we will transform our schools and colleges and universities to meet the demands of a new age. All this we can do. All this we will do.

MAJOR ACCOMPLISHMENTS

- ***Lilly Ledbetter Fair Pay Act*** restored basic protections against pay discrimination for women and other workers.

- ***American Recovery and Reinvestment Act*** focused on expanding the job market, spurring economic activity and investment, and fostering accountability and transparency in government.

It also included investment in computerized medical records and improvement of services to American's veterans.

- ***Children's Health Insurance Reauthorization Act*** provided quality health care to 11 million children, 4 million of whom were previously uninsured.
- ***Edward M. Kennedy Serve America Act*** increased the size of Americorps and created a Social Innovation Fund.
- ***Patient Protection and Affordable Care Act***, commonly known as health reform, made insurance more affordable, set up a competitive health insurance market, brought greater accountability to health care, and ended discrimination against Americans with pre-existing conditions.

Bibliography & Permissions

Allen, Charles F. and Jonathan Portis. *The Comeback Kid: The Life and Career of Bill Clinton.* New York: Carol Publishing Group, 1992.

Alsop, Joseph. *FDR 1882-1945: A Centenary Remembrance.* New York: Viking Press, 1982.

Asner, Edward. Personal communication, response to author's request.

Baker, Jean H. *The Stevensons: A Biography of an American Family.* New York: W. W. Norton & Co., 1996.

Baldacci, John E. Personal communication, response to author's request.

Boller, Paul F. Jr. *Presidential Campaigns* (Revised Edition). New York: Oxford University Press, 1996.

Burstein, Andrew. *The Passions of Andrew Jackson.* New York: Alfred A. Knopf, 2003.

Carter, James E. Jr. Nomination Acceptance Speech to the Democratic National Convention, July 16, 1976. Jimmy Carter Library.

Carter, James E. Jr. Inaugural Address, January 20, 1977. Jimmy Carter Library.

Chisholm, Shirley A. "Equal Rights for Woman." Address to the U. S. House of Representatives, May 21, 1969. *Congressional Record*, Extension of Remarks, E4165-6.

Clinton, William J. Nomination Acceptance Speech to the Democratic National Convention, July 16, 1992. William J. Clinton Library.

Clinton, William J. First Inaugural Address, January 20, 1993. William J. Clinton Library

Dallek, Robert. *An Unfinished Life: John F. Kennedy 1917 – 1963.* Boston: Little, Brown & Co., 2003.

Dittmer, John. *Local People: The Struggle for Civil Rights in Mississippi.* Urbana: University of Illinois Press, 1994.

Dukakis, Michael S. Nomination Acceptance Speech to the Democratic National Convention, July 21, 1988. Reprinted with the permission of The Honorable Michael Dukakis.

Ellis, Joseph J. *American Sphinx: The Character of Thomas Jefferson.* New York: Alfred A. Knopf, 1997.

Featured Legislation. whitehouse.gov/briefingroom/signed-legislation.

Feingold, Russell D. Statement from the Floor of the U. S. Senate on the Anti-Terrorism Bill, October 25, 2001. feingold.senate.gov.

Ford, Harold E. Jr. Keynote Address to the Democratic National Convention, August 15, 2000. Reprinted with the permission of The Honorable Harold E. Ford, Jr.

Garraty, John A. and Mark A. Carnes, editors. *American National Biography.* New York: Oxford University Press, 1999.

Glaser, Elizabeth. Address to Democratic National Convention, July 14, 1992. Reprinted with the permission of Paul Glaser.

Gore, Al. *Earth in the Balance.* New York: Houghton-Mifflin, 1992.

Gore, Al. Remarks at Glacier National Park, September 2, 1997. Clinton3/nara.gov/WH/EOP/OVP/speeches/glacier.

Gore, Al. *An Inconvenient Truth.* New York: Rodale, 2006.

Halliday, E. M. *Understanding Thomas Jefferson.* New York: Harper Collins Publishers, 2001.

Humphrey, Hubert H. Speaking on Behalf of the Minority Report on Civil Rights to the Democratic National Convention, July 14, 1948. Reprinted with the permission of The Hubert H. Humphrey Papers, Minnesota Historical Society.

Johnson, Lyndon B. The Great Society, University of Michigan, May 22, 1964. Lyndon Baines Johnson Library.

Johnson, Lyndon B. Special Message to the Congress: The American Promise, March 15, 1965. Lyndon Baines Johnson Library.

Jordan, Barbara C. "Who Then Will Speak for the Common Good?" Keynote Speech to the Democratic National Convention, July 12, 1976. Reprinted with the permission of Hilgers and Watkins, P.C. on behalf of the Barbara Jordan Estate.

Kearns, Doris. *Lyndon Johnson and the American Dream.* New York: Harper & Row, 1976.

Kennedy, David, Lizabeth Cohen, and Thomas A. Bailey. *The American Pageant,* 12th edition. New York: Houghlin Mifflin, 2002.

Kennedy, Edward M. Address to the Democratic National Convention, August 12, 1980. Reprinted with the permission of The Honorable Edward M. Kennedy.

Kennedy, John F. Nomination Acceptance Speech to the Democratic National Convention, July 15, 1960. John F. Kennedy Library.

Kennedy, John F. Inaugural Address, Washington, D. C., January 20, 1961. John F. Kennedy Library.

Kennedy, John F. Radio and Television Report to the American People on Civil Rights, June 11, 1963. John F. Kennedy Library.

Kennedy, Robert F. Address to the Democratic National Convention, August 27, 1964. John F. Kennedy Library.

Kennedy, Robert F. "Recapturing America's Moral Vision." University of Kansas, March 18, 1968. John F. Kennedy Library.

Kerry, John F. "A Right and Responsibility to Speak Out." Faneuil Hall, Boston, MA, April 22, 2006. Reprinted with the permission of The Honorable John F. Kerry.

King, Martin Luther Jr. "Letter from Birmingham Jail." April 16, 1963. Copyright 1963 Martin Luther King, Jr., copyright renewed 1991 Coretta Scott King. Reprinted by arrangement with the Estate of Martin Luther King Jr., c/o Writers House as agent for the proprietor, New York, NY.

King, Martin Luther Jr. "I Have a Dream." August 28, 1963. Copyright 1963 Martin Luther King, Jr., copyright renewed 1991 Coretta Scott King. Reprinted by arrangement with the Estate of Martin Luther King Jr., c/o Writers House as agent for the proprietor, New York, NY.

Lewis, John. Extensions of His Remarks on the Floor of the U. S. House of Representatives on the Department of Peace and Nonviolence Act, February 7, 2007. johnlewis.house.gov

McCullough, David. *Truman.* New York: Simon & Schuster, 1992.

Mieczkowski, Yanek. *The Routledge Historical Atlas of Presidential Elections.* New York: Routledge, 2001.

Mondale, Walter F. Nomination Acceptance Speech to the Democratic National Convention, July 19, 1984. Reprinted with the permission of The Honorable Walter Mondale.

Obama, Barack H. Opening Statement from the Floor of the U.S. Senate on Ethics Reform," March 7, 2006. obama.senate.gov.

Obama, Barack H. Inaugural Address, January 20, 2009. whitehouse.gov.

Richards, Ann W. Address to the Democratic National Convention, July 18, 1988. Reprinted with the permission of The Honorable Ann Richards.

Rogers, Mary Beth. *Barbara Jordan: American Hero.* New York: Bantam Books, 1998.

Roosevelt, Eleanor. Speech to the American Civil Liberties Union, March 14, 1940. Franklin D. Roosevelt Library.

Roosevelt, Franklin D. Nomination Acceptance Speech to the Democratic National Convention, July 2, 1932. Franklin D. Roosevelt Library.

Roosevelt, Franklin R. Annual Address to Congress, January 6, 1941. Franklin D. Roosevelt Library.

Roosevelt, Franklin R. Address to the International Brotherhood of Teamsters, Chauffeurs, Warehousemen, and Helpers of America, September 23, 1944. Franklin D. Roosevelt Library.

Schulke, Flip and Penelope McPhee. *King Remembered.* New York: Simon & Schuster, 1986.

Stevenson, Adlai E. "Nature of Patriotism." Speech to the American Legion Convention, August 27, 1952. Reprinted with the permission of the Seeley G. Mudd Manuscript Library, Princeton University.

Thomas, Evan. *Robert Kennedy: His Life.* New York:

Simon & Schuster, 2000.

Truman, Harry S. Whistle-Stop Campaign Speech, Elizabeth, New Jersey, October 7, 1948. Truman Library.

Truman, Harry S. State of the Union Message, January 5, 1949. Truman Library.

Udall, Stewart L. Speech to the School of Forestry, University of California, Berkeley, April 19, 1963. Reprinted with the permission of the University of Arizona Library, Special Collections.

Wiesel, Elie. "The Perils of Indifference." Speech to a White House Symposium, April 12, 1999. Reprinted with the permission of Dr. Elie Wiesel.

Witcover, Jules. *Party of the People: The Democrats, a History.* New York: Random House, 2003.

INDEX

About the Author

Mary Ellen Andriot Blencoe grew up in the Virginia suburbs of Washington, D.C., where politics is a part of daily life. She first became actively involved in the Democratic Party during the 1964 Presidential campaign. She has been a lifelong Democrat, and recently has served at the county level as president of the Democratic women's club and secretary of the Democratic executive committee. In addition, she was a co-commentator for three years on *The Point*, a local political call-in television show. She graduated from Indiana University, and has 42 years of administrative experience in all levels of education – from pre-school through post-graduate – at the Wisconsin Department of Public Instruction, Stanford University, Pennsylvania State University, and two public school systems.

Made in the USA
Charleston, SC
02 May 2010